# Research Methods in Psychology

## (Students Study Guide)

By

## Suripeddi Koundinya

[M.A. Psychology
M.A. Astrology
M.Tech. Biotechnology]

**2022 JUNE**

# CONTENTS

# An Overview

The word **Research** is composed of two syllables, *re* and *search.* The dictionary defines the former as a prefix meaning again, a new or over again and the latter as a verb, meaning to examine closely and carefully, to test and try, or to probe.

Together they form a noun describing a careful, systematic, patient study and investigation in some field of knowledge, undertaken to establish facts or principles (Grinnell 1993). The simplest meaning of research is to search for facts, answers to research question and solution for the problem.

Research is a process through which new knowledge is discovered. Most Research is designed to draw the conclusion about the cause and effect relationship among the variables.

The goal of the research remains to develop a theory that explains the relationship found among variables.

This book is especially for Students who are preparing for competitive exams. A total of 44 questions with answers framed here followed as per the academic syllabus.

Visit Blog: https://psychologistera.blogspot.com/

## 1. Define Research? What are the criteria for conducting a good research?

Scientific Research is a systematic and objective attempt to provide answers to certain questions. The purpose of scientific research is to discover and develop an organised body of knowledge. Therefore, scientific research may be defined as the systematic and empirical analysis and recording of controlled observation, which may lead to the development of theories, concepts, generalisations and principles, resulting in prediction and control of those activities that may have some cause-effect relationship.

Some of the definitions of research in literature are given below which can help you to understand proper meaning and concept of research.

Encyclopaedia of Social Science defines research as, "the manipulation of generalising to extend, connect or verify knowledge…" Manipulation incorporates experimentation adopted for the purpose of arriving at generalisation.

*Kerlinger (1973)* defines research as a "systematic, controlled, empirical and critical investigation of hypothetical propositions about the presumed relationship about various phenomena."

*Burns (1994)* also defines research as 'a systematic investigation to find answers to a problem'.

According to *Clifford Woody*, Research comprises defining and redefining problems, formulating hypothesis or suggested solutions; collecting, organising and evaluating data; making deductions and reaching conclusions and at last carefully testing the conclusions to determine whether they fit the formulating hypothesis.

*D. Slesinger and M. Stephenson* in the Encyclopaedia of Social Sciences define Research as "the manipulation of things concepts or symbols for the purpose of generalising to extend, correct or verify knowledge aids in construction of theory or in the practice of an art.

Thus, the term research refers to the systematic method consisting of enunciating the problem, formulating a hypothesis, collecting the facts or data, analysing the facts and reaching certain conclusions either in the form of solution (s) towards the concerned problem or in certain generalisations for some theoretical formulation.

The Criteria for Good Research are as follows:
    a)  Purpose of research should be clearly defined and common concepts that are used should be operationally defined.

b) The research procedure should be precisely planned, focused and appropriately described in order to enable other researcher to do research for further advancement.

c) Research design should be carefully planned to generate results to maintained objectivity.

d) The research report should be as much as possible frank enough to gauge effects of the findings.

e) Data analysis in the research report should be adequate to reveal its significance and the method of analysis employed be appropriate and

f) Validity and reliability of data should be examined carefully.

Objectives / Purpose of a Good Research:

The purpose of research is to discover answers to questions through the application of scientific procedures. The main aim of research is to find out the truth which is hidden and which has not been discovered as yet. Though each research study has its own specific purpose, we may think of research objectives as falling into a number of following broad groupings:

a) To gain familiarity with a phenomenon or to achieve new insights into it (studies with this object in view are termed as exploratory research studies);

b) To portray accurately the characteristics of a particular individual, situation or group (studies with this object in view are known as descriptive research studies);

c) To determine the frequency with which something occurs or with which it is associated with something else (studies with this object in view are known as diagnostic research studies)'

d) To test a hypothesis of a causal relationship between variables (such studies are known as hypothesis-testing research studies/experimental studies).

Thus, research is the fountain of knowledge for the sake of knowledge and an important source of providing guidelines for solving different business, personal, profession governmental and social problems. It is a sort of formal training which enables one to understand the new developments in one's field in a better way.

2. **Write a short note on "qualities of good research"?**

Some of the main characteristics of good research are:

a) <u>**Operationism**</u>: this means labelling variables. The researcher must be able to label the independent, dependent and secondary variables appropriately.

Stanovich's (1989, p.39) defines it thus: "operationism is simply the idea that concepts in scientific theory must in some way be grounded in, or linked to, observable events that can be measured".

b) <u>**Empirical Observation and Evidence**</u>: it implies that any conclusion drawn is based upon hard core evidence gathered from information collected from real life experiences and observations. This provides a basis for external ability to research results.

c) <u>**Testability**</u>: This means that every research must be testable for it to be regarded as a good research.

d) <u>**Parsimony and Precision**</u> are two things that guide scientific research and make researches robust. Parsimony simply implies that ideas are not to be organised loosely.

e) **Scientific Basis**: Every research must have a scientific basis for it to be good. There must be clearly stated procedures with definite pathways of expected results.

f) **Being Systematic**: To be systematic, the research must follow a definite procedure such that any other researcher following the same approach would arrive at the results. This characteristic makes research a process of creating knowledge.

g) **Falsifiability:** According to Karl Popper, "what distinguishes a scientific theory from the unscientific one is the principle of refutability".

h) **Ethical Principles**: A good research must follow the ethical principles outlined by the discipline or by anybody or agency that sees to the conduct of researches.

i) **Replicable**: the designs, procedures and results of scientific research should be replicable so that any person other than the researcher himself may assess their validity.

## 3.  Elucidate the various steps involved in Research process?

Research process consists of series of actions and steps needed for conducting scientific research, if the researcher follows certain steps in conducting the research, the work can be carried out smoothly with least difficulty. These steps are described as beneath—

**Step-I:** *Identification of the Problem:*

The first and most important step for identifying a problem is asking a question or identifying a need that arises as a result of curiosity and to which it become necessary to find an answer. The psychological studies are focused on one or many of the following kinds of questions:

What are the events that cause or determine a given behaviour or response? What is the nature of behaviour or action (i.e., its structure) and how it is linked with other actions and behaviours?
What are the relationships of internal psychological processes with behavioural phenomenon?

The research question determines the direction of study and researchers have to struggle a lot in identifying and articulating the same. Essentially two steps are involved in formulating the research problem, viz, understanding the problem thoroughly, and rephrasing the same into meaningful terms.

The main function of formulating a research problem is to decide what you want to find out about.

**Step-II: _Formulating a Hypothesis_:**

When the researcher has identified the problem and reviewed the relevant literature he formulates a hypothesis which is a kind of suggested answer to the problem.

Hypothesis plays the key role in formulating and guiding any study. The hypotheses are generally derived from earlier research findings existing theories, and personal observations and experiences. From a careful examination of relevant theory and previous findings, the psychologist would be able to state one or more prepositions whose validity could be tested.

Hypothesis may be defined as a tentative statement showing a relationship between variables under study. It is stated in the form of a declarative sentence. For instance suppose you are interested to know the effect of reward on learning.

_Those who are rewarded shall require lesser number of trials to learn the lesson than those who are not rewarded._ For unbiased research the researcher must formulate a hypothesis in advance of the data – gathering process. No hypothesis should be formulated after the data are collected.

**Step-III: _Identifying, Manipulating and Controlling Variables_**

While talking about the hypothesis you will encounter this word i.e. variable in the scientific literature in the psychology. Variables are defined as those characteristics which are manipulated, controlled and observed by the experimenter.

At least three types of variables must be recognised at the outset -the dependent variable, the independent variable and the extraneous variable.

a) The **_Dependent variable_** is one about which the prediction is made on the basis of the experiment. In the other words the dependent variable is the characteristics or condition that changes as the experimenter changes the independent variables.

b) The **_Independent variable_** is that condition or characteristics which is manipulated or selected by the experimenter is order to find out its relationship to some observed phenomena.

c) An **_Extraneous variable_** is the uncontrolled variable that may affect the dependent variable. The experimenter is not interested in the changes, produced due to the extraneous variable and hence, he tries to control it as far as practicable. The extraneous variable is known as the relevant variable

**Step-IV: _Formulating a Research Design_**

A research design may be regarded as the blueprint of those procedures which are adapted by the researcher for testing the relationship between the dependent variable and the independent variable.

There are several kinds of experimental designs and the selection of any one is based upon the purpose of the research, types of variables to be controlled and manipulated as well as upon the conditions under which the experiment is to be conducted.

The main purpose of experimental design is to help the researcher in manipulating the independent variables freely and to provide maximum control of the extraneous variables so that it may be said with all certainty that the experimental change is due to only the manipulation of the experimental variable. The main function of a research design is to explain how you will find answers to your research questions.

The research design sets out the logic of your inquiry. A research design should include the following; logistical arrangements have to made according to proposed research design , the measurement procedures, the sampling strategy, the frame of analysis and the time frame.

For any investigation, the selection of an appropriate research design is crucial in enabling you to arrive at valid findings, comparisons and conclusions.

## Step-V: _Constructing Devices for Observation and Measurement_

When the research design has been formulated, the next step is to construct or choose appropriate tools of research for scientific observation and measurement.

Questionnaire and interview schedule are the most common tools which have been developed for the psychological research. If the readymade tools are not available then the researcher may have develop appropriate tools before undertaking the study.

All these tools of research are ways through which data are collected by asking for information from person rather than observing them.

### Step-VI: _Sample Selection and Data Collection_

After deciding the tools for the study the researcher also decides about the participants of the study. Usually a small sample is drawn which represents the population.

The participants could be children, adolescents, college students, teachers, managers, clinical patients or any group of the individual in whom/ where the phenomenon under investigation is prevalent.

Depending on the nature of research problem a researcher may choose particular method (e.g. observation, experiment, case study, and survey) for data collection. The researcher also decides how the tools to be administered to collect data that is individual or group.

### Step-V: _Data Analysis and their Interpretation_

After making observation the data collected are analysed with the help of various quantitative / statistical and qualitative techniques.

Careful scrutiny of the data is a critical aspect of scientific method. The purpose of the analysis is to make sense of the data and see what light they throw on the problem and the hypotheses of the study and draws conclusion accordingly. Data analysis can be done by using univariate analysis in which research deals with a single characteristics of interest, bivariate analysis in which researcher deals with two characteristics of interest and by using multivariate analysis in which more than two characteristics are involves.

Depending upon the nature of data and purpose of the experiment, either a parametric statistic or a non-parametric statistic is chosen for statistical analysis.

In general, the purpose of carrying out the statistical analysis is to reject the null hypothesis so that the alternative hypothesis may be accepted.

**Step-VI: _Drawing Conclusions_**

The investigator, after analysing the results, draws some conclusions. In fact the investigator wants to make some statement about the research about the research problem which he could not make without conducting his research. Whatever conclusion drawn, researcher generalises it to the whole population. During this phase, hypotheses are accepted or rejected. At the same time the conclusions of the study are related to the theory or research findings from which the hypotheses originally came. Depending on the new findings the original theory may have to be modified.

**Step-VII:** *Preparation of Report and Publication*

This is the last step in most of the research studies. The researcher documents all the steps of his or her research in clear terms this report inform that what you have done, what you have discovered and what conclusion you have drawn from findings. If you are clear about the whole process you will also be clear about the way you want to write in your report. This helps the reader to understand the study and use it for various purposes.

## 4. Explain the concept of Reliability? What are the different methods of estimating reliability?

Most research is designed to draw the conclusion about the cause and effect relationship among the variables. The goal of the research remains to develop a theory that explains the relationship found among variables.

There are two goals of research design;

a) Obtain information relevant to the purposes of the study.
b) Collect this information with maximal reliability and validity.

Reliability is the consistency of your measurement, or the degree to which an instrument measures the same way each time it is used under the same condition with the same subjects. In short, it is the repeatability of measurement.

A measure is considered reliable if a person's score on the same test given twice is similar. It is important to remember that reliability is not measured, it is estimated. For instance, if a test is constructed to measure a particular trait; say, neuroticism, then each time it is administered, it should yield same results. A test is considered reliable if we get same result repeatedly.

According to *Anastasi (1957)*, the reliability of test refers to the consistency of scores obtained by the individual on different occasions or with different sets of equivalent items.

According to *Stodola and Stordahl (1972)*, the reliability of a test can be defined as the correlation between two or more sets of scores of equivalent tests from the same group of individuals.

According to *Guilford (1954)*, reliability is the proportion of the true variance in obtained test scores.

There are number of ways of estimating reliability of an instrument. Various procedures can be classified into two groups:

A) External consistency procedures
B) Internal consistency procedures

## A) External Consistency Procedures:

External consistency procedures compare findings from two independent process of data collection with each other as a means of verifying the reliability of the measure. Two methods are as beneath.

### a) *Test Re-test Reliability:*

Test-Retest reliability is estimated, when same test is administered on same sample. Therefore, if refers to the consistency of a test among on two different time periods different administrations.

The reliability coefficient in this case would be the correlation between the score obtained by the same person on two administrations of the test.

The reliability coefficient in this case would be the correlation between the score obtained by the same person on two administrations of the test.

i) **Memory effect /carry over effect:** One of the common problems with test-retest reliability is that of memory effect. This argument particularly holds true when, the two administrations takes place within short span of time, for example, when a memory related experiment including nonsense syllables is conducted whereby, the subjects are asked to remember a list in a serial wise order, and the next experiment is conducted within 15 minutes, most of the times, subject is bound to remember his/her responses, as a result of which there can be prevalence of artificial reliability coefficient since subjects give response from memory instead of the test. Same is the condition when pre-test and post-test for a particular experiment is being conducted.

**ii) Practice effect:** This happens when repeated tests are being taken for the improvement of test scores, as is typically seen in the case of classical IQ where there is improvement in the scores as we repeat these tests.

iii) **Absence:** People remaining absent for re-tests.

b)  *Parallel Forms Reliability:*

Parallel-Forms Reliability is known by the various names such as Alternate forms reliability, equivalent form reliability and comparable form reliability.

Parallel forms reliability compares two equivalent forms of a test that measure the same attribute. The two forms use different items. However, the rules used to select items of a particular difficulty level are the same. When two forms of the test are available, one can compare performance on one form versus the other. Sometimes the two forms are administered to the same group of people on the same day.

The Pearson product moment correlation coefficient is used as an estimate of the reliability.

## **B)** Internal Consistency Procedures:

The idea behind internal consistency procedures is that items measuring same phenomena should produce similar results. Following internal consistency procedures are commonly used for estimating reliability-

### *a)* *Split Half Reliability*

In this method, as the name implies, we randomly divide all items that intends to measure same construct into two sets .The complete instrument is administered on sample of people and total scores are calculated for each randomly divided half; the split half reliability is then, the simply the correlation between these two scores.

A problem with this approach is that when the tests are shorter, they run the risk of losing reliability and it can most safely be used in case of long tests only. It is, hence, more useful in case of long tests as compared to shorter ones. However to rectify the defects of shortness, Spearman- Brown's formula can be employed, enabling correlation as if each part were full length:

R = (2rhh)/(1+rhh) (where rhh = correlation between 2 halves) *b)* **Kudar-Richardson Estimate of Reliability**

The coefficient of internal consistency could also be obtained with the help of Kudar-Richardson formula number 20. One of the techniques for item analysis is item difficulty index. Item difficulty is the proportion or percentage of those answering correctly to an item.

For example – symbol 'p' is used to represent the difficulty index. Suppose an item 'X' has p=0.67.this means item 'X' was answered correctly by 74% of those who answered the item.

To compute reliability with the help of Kuder-Richardson formula number 20, the following formula is used:

$$KR\text{-}20 = \frac{N}{N-1}\left[1 - \frac{\Sigma\,pq}{\sigma^2}\right]$$

Where
N = the number of items on the test,
$\sigma2$ = the variance of scores on the total test,
p = the proportion of examinees getting each item correct,
q = the proportion of examinees getting each item wrong.

Kuder-Richardson formula 20 is an index of reliability that is relevant to the special case where each test item is scored 0 or 1 (e.g., right or wrong).

## c)  Cronbach's Alpha ($\alpha$)

As proposed by Cronbach (1951) and subsequently elaborated by others (Novick & Lewis, 1967; Kaiser & Michael, 1975), coefficient alpha may be thought of as the mean of all possible split-half coefficients, corrected by the Spearman-Brown formula . The formula for coefficient alpha is

$$r_{\alpha} = \left( \frac{N}{N-1} \right) \left( 1 - \frac{\Sigma \sigma^2_j}{\sigma^2} \right)$$

Where $r\alpha$ is coefficient alpha

N is the no. of items.

$\sigma^2_j$ is the variance of one item.

$\Sigma\sigma^2_j$ is the sum of variances of all items, and

$\sigma^2$ is the variance of the total test scores.

As with all reliability estimates, coefficient alpha can vary between 0.00 and 1.00.

## 5.  Write short notes on types of Validity?

Validity refers to the degree to which a test measures, what it claims to measure. It is very necessary for a test to be valid for its proper administration and interpretation.

According to Standard for Educational and Psychological testing (AERA, APA & NCME 1985, 1999); a test is valid to the extent that inferences drawn from it are appropriate, meaningful and useful. According to Cronbach (1951) validity is the extent to which a test measures what it purports to measure.

According to Freeman (1971) an index of validity shows the degree to which a test measures what it purports to measure when compared with accepted criteria.

According to Anastasi (1988) the validity of a test concerns what the test measures and how well it does so.

There are six types of validity, viz., (i) Content validity (ii) Criterion-related validity (iii) Con current validity (iv) Predictive validity (v) Construct validity (vi) Convergent validity (vii) Discriminate validity and (viii) Face validity.

## i) Content Validity:

According to Mc Burney and White (2007); content validity is the notion that a test should sample range of behaviour that is represented by the theoretical concept being measured.

It is a non-statistical type of validity with involvement of assessment of the content of the test to ascertain whether it includes the sample representative of the behaviour that is intended to be measured.

## ii) Criterion-related Validity:

Criterion related validity is the idea that a valid test should relate closely to other measure of the same theoretical concept. A valid test of intelligence should correlate highly with other intelligence test. If a test demonstrates effective predicting criterion or indicators of the construct, it is said to possess criterion – related validity.

There are two different types of criterion validity-

*a)* **Concurrent Validity:** Its occurrence is found when criterion measures are achieved at the same time as the test scores. It reflects the degree to which the test scores estimate the individual's present status with regards to criterion. For instance, if a test measures anxiety, it would be said to have concurrent validity if it rightly reflects the current level of anxiety experienced by an individual. Concurrent evidence of test validity is usually desirable for achievement tests and diagnostic clinical test.

*b)* **Predictive Validity:** occurs when criterion measures are obtained at a time after the test. For example, aptitude tests are useful in identifying who will be more likely to succeed or fail in a particular subject. Predictive validity is part curly relevant for entrance examination and occupational test.

### iii) <u>Construct Validity:</u>

Construct validity approach is complex than other forms of validity. Mc Burney and White (2007) defined construct validity as the property of a test that the measurement actually measures the constructs they are designed to measure.

There are several ways to determine whether a test generate data that have construct validity.

j)   The test should actually measure whatever theoretical construct it supposedly tests, and not something else. For example a test of leadership ability should not actually test extraversion.

k)   A test that has construct validity should measure what it intends to measure but not measure theoretically unrelated constructs. For example, a test of musical aptitude should not require too much reading ability.

l)   A test should prove useful in predicting results related to the theoretical concepts it is measuring. For example, a test of musical ability should predict who will benefit from taking music lessons, should differentiate groups who have chosen music as a career from those who haven't should relate to other tests of musical ability and so on.

There are two types of construct validity—'convergent validity' and 'divergent validity' (or discriminant validity).

a) ***Convergent Validity:*** It means the extent to which a measure is correlated with other measure which is theoretically predicted to correlate with.

b) ***Discriminant Validity:*** This explains the extent to which the operationalisation is not correlated with other operationalisations that it theoretically should not be correlated with.

## iv) <u>Face Validity:</u>

Face validity refers to what appears to measure superficially. It depends on the judgment of the researcher. Each question is scrutinised and modified until the researcher is satisfied that it is an accurate measure of the desired construct. The determination of face validity is based on the subjective opinion of the researcher.

## 6. Discuss the various threats of internal Validity?

Internal validity is the most fundamental type of validity because it concerns the logic of the relationships between the independent variable and dependent variable. This type of validity is an estimate of the degree to which inferences about causal relationship can be drawn, based on the measures employed and research design.

## Threats to Internal Validity

These include (i) confounding, (ii) selection bias, (iii) history, (iv) maturation, (v) repeated testing, (vi) instrument change, (vii) regression toward the mean, (viii) mortality, (ix) diffusion, (x) compensatory rivalry, (xi) experimenter bias.

i) *Confounding*: Confounding error that occurs when the effects of two variables in an experiment cannot be separated, resulting in a confused interpretation of the results. Confounding is one of the biggest threat to validity in experimentation. The problem of confounding is particularly acute in research in which the experimenter cannot control the independent variable. When participants are selected according to presence or absence of a condition, subject variable can affect the results. Where a false relationship cannot be avoided, a rival hypothesis may be developed to the original cause and inference hypotheses.

ii) *Selection bias*: Any bias in selecting a group can undermine internal validity. Selection bias indicates the problem that occurs as a result of its existence at the pre-test differences between groups, may interact with the independent variable and thus influence the observed outcome and creates problems; examples would be gender, personality, mental capabilities, and physical abilities, motivation level and willingness to participate.

iii)   *History*: Events outside the experiment or between repeated measures of dependent variables may influence participants' responses, attitudes and behaviour during process of experiment, like; natural disasters, political changes etc. In this condition, it becomes impossible to determine whether change in dependent variable is caused by independent variable or historical event.

iv)   *Maturation:* Usually, it happens that subjects change during the course of an experiment or between measurements. For instance, in longitudinal studies young kids might grow up as a result of their experience, abilities or attitudes which are intended to be measured. Permanent changes [such as physical growth] and temporary changes [like fatigue and illness] may alter the way a subject would react to the independent variable. Thus, researcher may have trouble in ascertaining if the difference is caused by time or other variables.

v)   *Repeated testing*: Participants may be driven to bias owing to repeated testing. Participants may remember correct answers or may be conditioned as a result of incessant administration of the test. Moreover, it also causes possibility of threat to internal validity.

vi) *Regression toward the mean*: During the experiment, if subjects are selected on the basis of extreme scores, then there are chances of occurrence of such an error. For example, when subjects with minimum mathematical abilities are chosen, at the end of the study if there is any improvement chances are that it would be due to regression towards the mean and not due to effectiveness of the course.

vii) *Mortality*: It should be kept in mind that there may be some participants who may have dropped out of the study before its completion. If dropping out of participants leads to relevant bias between groups, alternative explanation is possible that account for the observed differences.

viii) *Diffusion*: It might be observed that there will be a lack of differences between experimental and control groups if treatment effects spread from treatment groups to control groups. This, however, does not mean that, independent variable will have no effect or that there would not be a relationship between dependent and independent variable.

*ix)*      <u>*Compensatory rivalry/resentful demoralisation:*</u> There will be a change in the behaviour of the subject if the control groups alter as a result of the study. For instance, control group participants may work extra hard to see that expected superiority of the experimental group is not demonstrated. Again, this does not imply that the independent variable created no effect or that there would be no relationship between dependent and independent variable. Vice-versa, changes in the dependent variable may only be effected due to a demoralised control group, working less hard or demotivated.

*x)*      <u>*Experimenter bias:*</u> Experimenter bias happens while experimenters, without any intention or reluctance, behave differently to the participants of control and experimental groups that in turn, affect the results of the experiment. Experimental bias can be reduced by keeping the experimenter from knowing the condition in the experiment or its purpose and by standardising the procedure as much as possible.

## 7. Discuss various threats of External Validity?

According to McBurney and White (2007), external validity concerns whether results of the research can be generalised to another situation, different subjects, settings, and times and so on.

External validity lacks from the fact that experiments using human participants often employ small samples collected from a particular geographic location or with idiosyncratic features (e.g. volunteers). Because of this, it cannot be made sure that the conclusions drawn about cause-effect-relationships are actually applicable to the people in other geographic locations or in the absence of these features.

**Threat to External Validity**
How one may go wrong in making generalisations, is one of the major threats to external validity. Usually, generalisations are limited when the cause (i.e. independent variable) is dependent upon other factors; as a result, all the threats to external validity interact with the independent variable.

a) *Aptitude-Treatment-Interaction*: The sample might have some features that may interact with the independent variable causing to limit generalisability, for instance, conclusions drawn from comparative psychotherapy studies mostly use specific samples (example; volunteers, highly depressed, hardcore criminals).

b) *Situations*: All the situational factors, for example, treatment conditions, light, noise, location, experimenter, timing, scope and degree of measurement etc., may limit generalisations.

c) *Pre-Test Effects*: When the cause-effect relationships can only be found out after the pre-tests are carried out, then, this also tends to limit the generality of the findings.

d) *Post-Test Effects*: When cause-effect relationships can only be explored after the post-tests are carried out, then this can also be a cause for limiting the generalisations of the findings.

e) *Rosenthal Effects*: When derivations drawn from the cause-consequence relationships cannot be generalised to other investigators or researchers.

## 8. Discuss various types of Variables?

A variable, as the name implies, is something that varies. Webster says that a variable is "a thing that is changeable" or "a quantity that may have a number of different values." True, a variable is something that has at least two values: however, it is also important that the values of the variable be observable.

*Kerlinger* (1986) defined variable 'a property that taken as different values'.

According to *to D'Amato* (1970) variables may be defined as those attributes of objects, events, things and beings, which can be measured.

According to *Postman and Egan* (1949) a variable is a characteristic or attribute that can take on a number of values, for example, number of items that an individual solves on a particular test, the speed with which we respond to a signal, IQ, sex, level of anxiety, and different degree of illumination are the examples of variables that are commonly employed in psychological research.

**Types of Variables**:

## A) Stimulus, Organism and Response Variables

Psychologists are interested in studying the behaviour or causes of behaviour as variables. Many psychologists have adopted a theoretical viewpoint or model called the **S-O-R** model to explain all behaviour.

The symbols **S, O,** and **R** represent different categories of variables.

**S** is the symbol of stimuli, and the category may be referred to in general as stimulus variables. A stimulus variable is some form of energy in the environment, such as light, to which the organism is sensitive.

**O** is the symbol for organism variables, that is the changeable physiological and psychological characteristics of the organisms being observed.

Examples of such variables are anxiety level, age and heart rate etc.

Finally, **R** is the symbol for response and, in general, response variables, which refer to some behaviour or action of the organism like pressing a lever, and reaction to any stimulus, are the examples of responses variables.

You can understand an application of **S-O-R** model through the following example.

Suppose that an experiment is conducted in which a rat is placed on a metal grid floor, the grid is electrified, and the length of time it takes the rat to jump from the grid to a platform is measured. Using the **S-O-R** model, the electrical shock would be called a stimulus variable. The intensity of shock would be the value of the variable. The particular state of the organisms would be measured by the organismic variables. For example, the skin resistant of the rat at the time of shock was introduced would be an organismic variables. A response variable would be the latency (i.e. the elapsed time between the onsets of the shock and when the rat reaches the platform).

## **B)** Independent and Dependent Variables

An *independent variable* or stimulus variable is that factor manipulated or selected by the experimenter in his attempt to ascertain its relationship to an observed phenomenon.

A *dependent variable* is the factor that appears, disappears, or varies as the experimenter introduces, removes or varies the independent variable. (Townsend,1953). The dependent variable is a measure of the behaviour of the subject. The dependent variable is the response that the person or animal makes. This response is generally measured using at least one of several different dimensions (Alberto & Troutman 2006).

The dimensions are –
(a) <u>Frequency</u> – Number of times that a particular behaviour occurs,
(b) <u>Duration</u> - the amount of time that behaviour lasts.
(c) <u>Latency</u> –the amount of time between and when the behaviour is actually performed (d) force – the intensity or strength of behaviour.

## C) <u>Extraneous and Confounded Variables</u>

Any and all other variables that may 'mask' the relationship between independent variable and dependent variable are known as **Extraneous Variables**.

*Extraneous variables* may directly affect the dependent variable or may combine with the independent variable to produce an affect. Therefore, extraneous variables must be controlled so that the experimenter can determine whether the dependent variable changes in relation to variation in the independent variable.

Extraneous variables are relevant in nature, and in experimental studies, they belong to three major types i.e., organismic variables, situational variables and sequential variables. The subject related variables include age, sex; intelligence, personality etc. are organismic variables. The situational variables include environmental variables operating in the experimental setting (e.g. noise, temperature, humidity) and variables related to the experimental task. The sequence related variables deal with sequence effects. They arise when participants in experiments are required to be tested in several conditions.

***Confounding variables*** is one that varies with the independent variable. While **Variables and Constructs** doing a study if we are not careful then two variables may get combined so that the effect of one cannot be separated from the effect of other. This is known as confounding.

For instance, if you conducted a study of the effect of television viewing on perception of violence and the experimental group contained only adolescents, whereas the control group only adults, the age of participants would be confounded with the independent variable under study. Confounding makes the conclusions of the study doubtful. It is, therefore, necessary that effort should be made to unconfined the variables.

## **D)** Active and Attribute Variables

Any variable that is manipulated is called *active variables*. Examples of active variables are reward, punishment, methods of teaching, creating anxiety through instructions and so on. *Attribute variable* is that variable which is not manipulated but measured by the experimenter. Variables that are human characteristics like intelligence, Aptitudes, sex, socio economic status, education, field dependence and need for achievement are the example of attributes variables.

The word 'attribute' is more accurate enough when used within animated objects or references. Organisations, institutions, groups, population and geographical areas have attributes. Organisations are variably productive; groups differ in cohesiveness; geographical areas vary widely in resources.

## E) Quantitative and Categorical Variables

*Quantitative variables* are one that varies in amount whereas categorical variables vary in kind. Speed of response, intensity of sound, level of Illumination, intelligence etc. are the example of quantitative variables and gender, race, religion are the example of categorical variables. Precise and accurate measurements are possible with the quantitative variables because they can be easily ordered in terms of increasing and decreasing magnitude

Categorical variables can be of three types: Constant, dichotomous and polytomous.

When a variable can have only one value or category, for example taxi, tree and water, it is known as a **constant variables**.

When a variable can have only two categories as in yes/no, good/bad and rich/poor, it is known as *dichotomous variables*.

When variables can be divided into more than two categories, for example: religion (Christian, Muslim, Hindu); political parties (Labor, Liberal, Democrat); and attitudes (strongly favorable, favorable, uncertain, unfavorable, strongly unfavorable), it is called a polytomous variable.

## **F)** Continuous Variables and Discrete Variables

Quantitative variables are further divided into two categories, namely, continuous variables and discrete variables.

A distinction between continuous and discrete variables is especially useful in planning of research and analysis of data.

A *Continuous variable* is one which is capable of being measured in any arbitrary degree of fineness or exactness. Age, height, intelligence, reaction time, etc., are some of the examples of a continuous variable. The age of the person can be measured in years, month and days. Thus, all such variables which can be measured in the smallest degree of fineness are called continuous variable.

The *Discrete variables* are those variables which are not capable of being measured in any arbitrary degree of fineness or exactness because the variables contain a clear gap. For example, the number of members in a family, no. of females in particular group, no of books in library and so on constitutes the examples of a discrete variable.

## 9. Discuss the various kinds of Constructs?

Constructs are the building blocks of theories, helping to explain how and why certain phenomena behave the way that they do .

Constructs are mental abstractions that we used to express the ideas, people, organisations, events / objects/things that we are interested in.

Constructs are way of bringing theory down to earth, helping to explain the different components of theories, as well as measure / observe their behaviours.

Although the terms 'concept' and 'construct' have distinction, but these have similar meanings too. Yet, there is an important distinction. A concept may be defined as any describable regularity of real or imagined events or objects (Bourne, Ekstrand, & Dominowski, 1971). A concept is a set of features connected by some rule (Hulse, Egeth, Deese 1980).

Constructs are created and used for a wide variety of reasons, but generally have two common characteristics.

a) First, the construct is a part of a theoretical framework and is related in various ways to other constructs.
b) Second, a construct usually operationally defined so as to allow its observation and measurement.

## Type of Constructs:

As Mac-Corquodale & Meehl, (1948) Indicated that there are two types of constructs which are often employed by psychologist and behavioural scientist:

A) Intervening variables
B) Hypothetical construct

A) An **Intervening Variable** is construct which is utilised as a summary term for a group of other construct; It has no meaning apart from context in which it is utilised. As you know, Clark Hull, a behaviourist who proposed hypothetical deductive method of learning, utilised intervening variables in the formation of the learning theory. Hull defined reaction potential as the combination of habit strength and drive (Hilgard & Bower, 1966).

Reaction potential is an intervening variable, since it only summarizes other constructs (habits strength and drive) and has meaning only in relation to them. An example of intervening variable is, hostility which is inferred from hostile and aggressive acts.

B) In contrast, a Hypothetical Construct is a theoretical term which is employed to describe something "real." That is, it is an intermediary which has tangible characteristics.

Habit strength, defined by Hull as the number of reinforced trials, is a hypothetical construct. As another example, the word "reflex" refers to certain readily observable characteristics. The patellar reflex or "knee jerk" occurs when a small force is sharply applied at the appropriate point on the knee.
The term "reflex" refers t the chain of events that occurs within the organism after the application of the stimulus and before the response. Hence, reflex is a hypothetical construct.

As a further example, suppose an equation could be developed which would tell us how much a person knows:

$$K = AC \times IQ$$

Where: **Variables and Constructs**
  K = knowledge
 AC = amount of conditioning
  IQ = intelligence

AC could be defined as the number of reinforced trials a person receives and IQ as that person's score on a standard intelligence test. K could be defined as being a function of AC and IQ.  Therefore, AC and IQ are hypothetical constructs (they describe something real and are defined directly by the operations that established them or by which they were measured).

On the other hand, K is an intervening variable (it has no meaning of its own, but only summarizes or stands for other constructs). However, if K were defined as the number of correct solutions a person achieved on the "knowledge test," then K would also be a hypothetical construct.

## 10. Define Hypothesis. What are the various characteristics of good hypothesis?

A Hypothesis is a preliminary or tentative explanation or postulate by the researcher of what the researcher considers the outcome of an investigation will be. It is an informed / educated guess. It indicates the expectations of the researcher regarding certain variables. It is the most specific way in which an answer to a problem can be stated.

"A Hypothesis is a proposition which can be put to test to determine validity" (Goode & Hatt).
According to Mcguigan (1990), 'a testable statement of a potential relationship between two or more variables, i.e. advance as potential solution to the problem'.

Kerlinger (1973) defined 'a hypothesis is a conjectural statement of the relation between two or more variables'.

When a hypothesis is formulated, the investigator must determine usefulness of the formulated hypothesis. There are several criteria or characteristics of a good research hypothesis.

Some of these characteristics are enumerated below:

a) A good hypothesis is in agreement with the observed facts.
b) A good hypothesis does not conflict with any law of nature, which is known to be true.
c) A good hypothesis is stated in the simplest possible term.
d) A good hypothesis permits of the application of deductive reasoning.
e) A good hypothesis shows very clear verbalisation.
f) A good hypothesis ensures that the methods of verification are under the control of the investigator.
g) A good hypothesis ensures that the sample of readily approachable.
h) A good hypothesis should have logical unity and comprehensiveness.

**11. Enumerate possible difficulties while formulation a good hypothesis? Explain Formulation of Hypothesis?**

Hypothesis plays a key role in formulation and guiding any study. The hypothesis is generally derived from earlier research findings, existing theories and personal observations as well as experiences.

A researcher should consider certain points while formulating a hypothesis:

a) Expected relationship or differences between variables.
b) Operational definition of variable.
c) Hypotheses are formulated following the review of literature.

By stating a specific hypothesis, the researcher narrows the focus of the data collection effort and is able to design a data collection procedure which is aimed at testing the plausibility of the hypothesis as a possible statement of the relationship between the terms of the research problem.

It is, therefore, always useful to have a clear idea and vision about the hypothesis. It is essential for the research question as the researcher intents to verify, as it will direct and greatly help to interpretation of the results.

***Possible Difficulties in Formulation of a Good Hypothesis***:

a) First, the absence of knowledge of a theoretical framework is a major difficulty in formulating a good research hypothesis.
b) Second, if detailed theoretical evidences are not available or if the investigator is not aware of the availability of those theoretical evidences, a research hypothesis cannot be formulated.
c) Third, when the investigator is not aware of the scientific research techniques, she/he will not be able to frame a good research hypothesis.

Despite these difficulties, the investigator attempts in her/his research to formulate a hypothesis. Usually the hypothesis is derived from the problem statement. The hypothesis should be formulated in a positive and substantive form before data are collected. In some cases additional hypothesis may be formulated after collection of data, but they should be tested on a new set of data and not on the old set which has suggested it. The formulation of a hypothesis is a creative task and involves a lot of thinking, imagination and innovation.

## 12. Elucidate various types of Hypothesis?

Hypotheses can be classified into several types, like; universal hypotheses, existential hypotheses, conceptual hypotheses etc. Broadly, there are two categories of the hypothesis:

i) Null hypothesis
ii) Alternative hypothesis

i) The **Null Hypothesis** is an important component of the decision making methods of inferential statistics. It is symbolised as $H_o$. If the difference between the samples of means is found significant the researcher can reject the null hypothesis. It indicates that the differences have statistically significant and acceptance of null hypothesis indicates that the differences are due to chance. Null hypothesis should always be specific hypothesis i.e. it should not state about or approximately a certain value.

Null hypothesis is useful tool in testing the significance of difference. In its simplest form, this hypothesis asserts that there is no true difference between two population means, and the difference found between sample means is, accidental and unimportant, that is arising out of fluctuation of sampling and by chance. Traditionally null hypothesis stated that there is zero relationship between terms of the hypothesis. For example,

(a) Schizophrenics and normal do not differ with respect to digit span memory.
(b) There is no relationship between intelligence and height.

If we want to test the hypothesis that the mean of the population to be taken as $\mu = \mu_0$.

ii)      **Alternative hypothesis** is symbolised as H1 or Ha, is the hypothesis that specifies those values that are researcher believes to hold true, and the researcher hopes that sample data will lead to acceptance of this hypothesis as true.

The alternative hypothesis is stated as follows:

$$H1: \mu \neq \mu_0$$

## 13. Write a short note on "Type I and Type II errors".

When a statistical hypothesis is tested, there are 4 possible results:

a) The hypothesis is true bit our test rejects it. (Type I error)
b) The hypothesis is false but our test accepts it. (Type II error)
c) The hypothesis is true but our test accepts it. (Correct Decision)
d) The hypothesis is false and our test rejects it. (Correct Decision)

Type I error – Rejection of a null hypothesis when it is true.
Type II error - Acceptance of a null hypothesis when it is false.

The sizes of Type-I error and Type-II error are denoted by $\alpha$ and $\beta$ respectively.

## 14. Detail on Sampling methods?

Sampling is the process of selection of units (e.g. people, organisation) from a population of interest so that by studying the sample may fairly generate results back to the population from which they were chosen.

According to Young (1992) "A statistical sample is miniature picture of cross selection of the entire group or aggregate from which the sample is taken".

According to Goode and Hatt (1981) "A sample, as the name implies, is a smaller representative of a large whole".

According to Blalock (1960) "It is a small piece of the population obtained by a probability process that mirrors with known precision, the various patterns and sub-classes of population".

***Sampling Terminology***:

a) **Population** is a well-defined set up of all elements pertaining to a given characteristic. It refers to the whole that include all observations or measurements of a given characteristic. Population is also called universe or population. It may be defined as any identifiable and well specified group of individual for example. All primary teachers, no number of all college teachers and all university students are the example of population. A population may be finite or infinite.

b) A **Sample** is any number of persons selected to represent the population according to some rule of plan. Thus, a sample is a smaller representation of the population. A measure based upon a sample is known as a statistic.

c) **Sample size**: No. of selected individual for example, no. of students, families from whom you obtain the require information is called the sample size and usually denoted by the letter (n).

d) ***Sampling design or strategy***: The way researcher selects the sample or students or families etc. is called the sampling design and strategy. It refers to the techniques or procedures the researcher would adopt in selecting some sampling units from which inferences about the population are drawn.

e) **Sampling unit**: Each individual or case that becomes the basis for selecting a sample is called sampling unit or sampling elements.

f) **Sampling frame**: The list of people from which the sample is taken. It should be comprehensive, complete and up-to-date. Examples of sampling frame: Electoral Register; Postcode Address File; telephone book.

**Purpose of Sampling**:

The objective of sampling is to derive the desired information about the population at the minimum cost or with the maximum reliability. Further, the aims in selecting a sample are to achieve maximum precision in estimates within a given sample size and to avoid bias in the selection of sample. Bias in the selection of sample can take place if: (a) the researcher selects the sample by non-random method and influenced by human choice. (b) The researcher does not cover the sampling population accurately and completely (c) A section of a sample population is impossible to find or refuses to cooperate.

**<u>Sampling Methods</u>:**

Blalock (1960) indicated that most sampling methods could be classified into two categories:

i) Non probability sampling methods
ii) Probability sampling methods

j) **<u>Non probability Sampling</u>** is one in which there is no way of assessing the probability of the element or group of elements, of population being included in the sample. In other words, non-probability sampling methods are those that provide no basis for estimating how closely the characteristics of sample approximate the parameters of population from which the sample had been obtained. This is because non probability sample do not use the techniques of random sampling.

Important techniques of non-probability sampling methods are:

a) **Haphazard, Accidental, or Convenience Sampling:**

Haphazard sampling can produce ineffective, highly unrepresentative samples and is not recommended. When a researcher haphazardly selects cases that are convenient, he or she can easily get a sample that seriously misrepresents the population. Such samples are cheap and quick; however, the systematic errors that easily occur make them worse than no sample at all. The person-on-the street interview conducted by television programs is an example of a haphazard sample.

### b) **Quota Sampling**:

Quota Sampling is an improvement over haphazard sampling. In quota sampling, a researcher first identifies relevant categories of people (e.g., male and female; or under age 30, ages 30 to 60, over age 60, etc.), then decides how many to get in each category. Thus, the number of people in various categories of the sample is fixed. For example, a researcher decides to select 5 males and 5 females under age 30, 10 males and 10 females aged 30 to 60, and 5 males and 5 females over age 60 for a 40-person sample. It is difficult to represent all population characteristics accurately.

### c) **Purposive Sampling:**

Purposive sampling is a valuable kind of sampling for special situations. It is used in exploratory research or in field research. It uses the judgment of an expert in selecting cases or it selects cases with a specific purpose in mind. With purposive sampling, he researcher never knows whether the cases selected represent the population. Purposive sampling is appropriate to select unique cases that are especially informative.

For example, a researcher wants to study the temperamental attributes of certain problem behaviour children.

### d) **Snowball Sampling**

Snowball sampling is also known as network, chain referral or reputation sampling method. Snowball sampling which is a non-probability sampling method is basically sociometrist. It begins by the collection of data on one or more contacts usually known to the person collecting the data. At the end of the data collection process (e.g., questionnaire, survey, or interview), the data collector asks the respondent to provide contact information for other potential respondents. These potential respondents are contacted and provide more contacts.

Snowball sampling is most useful when there are very few methods to secure a list of the population or when the population is unknowable.

Snowball sampling has some advantages—

1) Snowball sampling, which is primarily a sociometrist sampling technique, has proved very important and is helpful in studying small informal social group and its impact upon formal organisational structure,

2) Snowball sampling reveals communication pattern in community organisation concepts like community

power; and decision-making can also be studied with the help of such sampling technique.

Snowball sampling has some limitations also—

1) Snowball sampling becomes cumbersome and difficult when is large or say it exceeds 100,

2) This method of sampling does not allow the researcher to use probability statistical methods. In fact, the elements included in sample are not randomly drawn and they are dependent on the subjective choices of the originally selected respondents.

e)  **Systematic Sampling:**

Systematic sampling is another method of non-probability sampling plan, though the label 'systematic' is somewhat misleading in the sense that all probability sampling methods are also systematic sampling methods. Due to this, it often sounds that systematic sampling should be included under one category of probability sampling, but in reality this is not the case.

ii)      **Probability Sampling** methods are those that clearly specify the probability or likelihood of inclusion of each element or individual in the sample. Probability sampling is free of bias in selecting sample units. They help in estimation of sampling errors and evaluate sample results in terms of their precision, accuracy and efficiency and hence, the conclusions reached from such samples are worth generalisation and comparable to similar population to which they belong.

Major probability sampling methods are:

a) **Simple random sampling:**

A simple random sample is a probability sample. A simple random sample requires
(a) a complete listing of all the elements

(b) an equal chance for each elements to be selected

(c) a selection process whereby the selection of one element has no effect on the chance of selecting another element. For example, if we are to select a sample of 10 students from the seventh grade consisting of 40 students, we can write the names (or roll number) of each of the 40 students on separate slips of paper – all equal in size and colour – and fold them in a similar way.
Subsequently, they may be placed in a box and reshuffled thoroughly.

Advantages of simple random sampling are:
1) Each person has equal chance as any other of being selected in the sample.

2) Simple random sampling serves as a foundation against which other methods are sometimes evaluated.

3) It is most suitable where population is relatively small and where sampling frame is complete and up-to-date.

4) As the sample size increases, it becomes more representative of universe.

5) This method is least costly and easily assessable of accuracy.

Despite these advantages, some of the disadvantages are:

1) Complete and up-to-date catalogued universe is necessary.

2) Large sample size is required to establish the reliability.

3) When the geographical dispersion is so wider therefore study of sample item has larger cost and greater time.

4) Unskilled and untrained investigator may cause wrong results.

### b)  <u>Stratified random sampling</u>

In stratified random sampling the population is divided into two or more strata, which may be based upon a single criterion such as sex, yielding two strata-male and female, or upon a combination of two or more criteria such as sex and graduation, yielding four strata, namely, male undergraduates, male graduates, female undergraduates and female graduates. These divided populations are called subpopulations, which are non-overlapping and together constitute the whole population.

Having divided the population into two or more strata, which are considered to be homogeneous internally, a simple random sample for the desired number is taken from each population stratum. Thus, in stratified random sampling the stratification of population is the first requirement. There can be many reasons for stratification in a population.

Two of them are:
1) Stratification tends to increases the precision in estimating the attributes of the whole population.
2) Stratification gives some convenience in sampling. When the population is divided into several units, a person or group of person may be deputed to supervise the sampling survey in each unit.

Advantages of stratified Random Sampling are:
1) Stratified sampling is more representative of the population because formation of stratum and random selection of item from each stratum make it hard to exclude in strata of the universe and increases the sample's representation to the population or universe.
2) It is more precise and avoids the bias to great extent.
3) It saves time and cost of data collection since the sample size can be less in the method.

Despite these advantages, some of the disadvantages of stratified sampling are:

1) Improper stratification may cause wrong results.

2) Greater geographical concentration may result in heavy cost and more time.

3) Trained investigators are required for stratification.

## c) **Cluster sampling**

A type of random sample that uses multiple stages and is often used to cover wide geographic areas in which aggregated units are randomly selected and then sample are drawn from the sampled aggregated units or cluster

For example, if the investigator wanted to survey some aspect of 3rd grade elementary school going children. First, a random sample of number of states from the country would be selected. Next, within each selected state, a random selection of certain number of districts would be made. Then within district a random selection of certain number of elementary schools would be made. This sampling method is more flexible than the other methods. Sub-divisions at the second stage unit needs be carried out only those unit selected in the first stage. Despite these merits, this sampling method is less accurate than a sample, containing the same number of the units in single stage samples.

## 15. What is Survey Research Method? Discuss the steps involved in conducting survey research?

The term "Survey" can be defined as a process which may involve an investigation/ examination or assessment in the form of a short paper and-pencil feedback form to an intensive one-on-one in-depth interview. With the help of the questionnaire or other statistical tools, the method tries to gather data about people, their thoughts and behaviours.

The method of survey research is a non-experimental (that is, it does not involves any observation under controlled conditions), descriptive research method which is one of the quantitative method used for studying of large sample. In a survey research, the researcher collects data with the help of standardised questionnaires or interviews which is administered on a sample of respondents from a population (population is sometimes referred to as the universe of a study which can be defined as a collection of people or object which possesses at least one common characteristic).

**Step 1:** Determination of the aims and objectives of study:
The researcher must at the outset analyse and assess the relevant areas or issues which need to be studied. Once the research area is selected by the researcher, the basic aims and objectives have to be clearly specified. These have to be focused and analysed so as to make the purpose of research relevant and understandable. The researchers have to

come up with the basic aims and objectives which would be focused and analysed in their overall research.

**Step 2:** <u>Define the population to be studied:</u>

After selecting the theme of the research, the researcher also needs to define the target population which would be studied by him/her.

**Step 3:** <u>Design and construct a survey:</u>

Once the target population is defined by the researcher, he or she needs to design a survey research. On the basis of the framed design, the research decides to conduct a survey, selects instrument for survey (for example telephonic interview) with the help of which data will be collected. After the selection of the instrument, the researcher conducts a pilot study (a small survey taken in advance of a major investigation or research). The pilot study helps the researcher to analyse the significance and relevance of the instruments selected by the researcher for the present research.

**Step 3:** <u>Select a representative sample:</u>

The process of construction of the survey instruments gives a way to the selection of the sample from the target population. The researcher selects a sample which represents nearly maximum characteristics of the whole universe/ population

**Step 4:** <u>Administer the survey:</u>

After the selection of the sample, the researcher conducts the survey by administering the survey instrument or tool on the selected sample. This step helps in the collection of the required data or information from the sample.

**Step 5:** <u>Analyse and interpret the findings of the survey</u>:

Once the data has been collected, the researcher analyses the data with the help of required statistical tools and then interprets the findings on the basis of the information revealed. This step involves several processes such as coding the data and then processing it.

**Step 6:** <u>Prepare the report of the survey</u>:

On the basis of the analysis and interpretation of the results, the researcher prepares a report of the overall research conducted. The report contains all the details of aims, objectives, data analysis, interpretation and discussion of the results. In this step, the researcher tries to evaluate how the findings meet the proposed aims and objectives of the research.

**Step 7:** <u>Communicate the findings of the survey</u>:

The most important step of conducting the survey research is to disseminate the survey findings. The researcher needs to communicate the findings to the target population and it is equally important record for the future research to be done on a similar field. The impacts of the survey results are also assessed on them, on the basis of which the researcher may also recommend certain policies on decision making.

## 16. What are the methods or instruments used in collecting data through Survey Research?

The tools used for data collection through survey research are aimed at obtaining information in a consistent way for all participants in the survey.

a) **Sampling**: A Sample is a representative of the Population or Universe selected for study. The technique of sampling can in itself act as an instrument in collecting data in survey research. For example if the researcher wants to study the level of job satisfaction amongst the employees of an organisation, then the researcher can select and study the attitude of at least ten persons of each department of the organisation. In order to avoid any bias, the sampling can be done with the help of randomisation (a method of sampling which provides an equal chance for each subject to be involved in the study, which can be done with the help of lottery or fish bowl technique) or stratification (a method of sampling which categorizes the population in to various categories and subcategories and then conducting the research).

b) **Questionnaire:** Questionnaires are basically a kind of paper pencil and multiple choice test in which the individual needs to select the most suitable alternative. The researcher may collect data with the help of a questionnaire from a large number of samples at a single time.

Questionnaires can be administered to the sample in three ways: (i) Mail survey (ii) Group administered questionnaire and (iii) household drop off survey. These are being discussed in detail below:

i) *Mail survey*: The researcher may forward a soft copy of the questionnaire to a large number of respondents through mail and can get the data collected from them at a single time. It is one of the relatively inexpensive, less time consuming and convenient method of getting responses. Yet, the questions which require on the spot response or detailed answer is difficult to be achieved through mail survey.

ii) *Group administered questionnaire*: It is one of the traditional methods of administering questionnaire. The researcher calls for a large number of respondents to be present at a stipulated time period as a group.
Under such group settings, the respondents are asked to respond to a structured sequence of questions written in paper or questionnaire. The greatest advantage of this method is that the respondents can clarify their doubt regarding any questioned that has been asked by the researcher instantly.

iii) *Household drop-off survey*: In this method, the researcher goes door to door to the respondents and personally hands over as well as collects the questionnaire from them. It is a kind of pick and drop facility which is provided by the researcher so that the researcher can answer the questions according to their convenience.

c) **Interview:** Interview is a kind of face to face interaction which helps in providing more honest answers and responses from the sample, as the interviewer (the one who is interviewing i.e., the researcher) works directly with the respondent or the interviewee (the one who is being interviewed).

Unlike questionnaires, the interviewer has an opportunity to ask follow-up questions. They are the best suitable methods for those questions which require opinions or impressions from the respondents.

Interviews can be of different types as given below:

i) *Structured interview:* Structured interviews are those interviews in which the questions that are to be asked from the respondents are prepared and pre-planned in advance by the researcher. The researcher imposes those prepared questions on the respondents serially and notes down the answers given by them.

ii) *Unstructured interview:* Interviews are said to be unstructured when the researcher conducts an interaction with the respondent in an informal atmosphere.

Nothing is pre-planned in advance. The response of the sample gives a clue to the researcher to ask the next question.

iii) *Telephonic interview*: In order to save time and money, the researcher may call the subjects or sample through telephone and ask them questions to collect data. This method helps in saving time and energy but the sample gets limited to only that part of the population who have the facility of telephones at their residences or offices.

## 17. Discuss the various kinds of Survey Research?

Based on the selection of an instrument or method of data collection, the researcher can use qualitative (e.g. ask open-ended questions) or quantitative (e.g. use forced choice questions) measures.

Basically there are two major types of survey:
Cross sectional surveys and longitudinal surveys, though there exist some other types of surveys also. These are explained below:

### A) Cross Sectional Survey:

Cross sectional surveys are used by the researcher when he or she wants to collect data from varied or different types of groups ( that may be in terms of age, sex, group, nation, tribes and so on) at a single time. An example of such a survey can be a study on the effect of socialisation of children of different age groups of a particular country. This type of survey is less time consuming and economical as well.

### B)  Longitudinal survey

This type of research is used only when the subject wants to study the same sample for a longer period of time. Such longitudinal studies may be used to study behavioural changes, attitude changes, religious effects or any event or practice that may have a long time effect on the selected sample or population.

There are three main types of longitudinal studies which help the researcher to analyse the long term effects on the selected sample.

These three include (i) Trend studies (ii) Cohort studies and (iii) Panel studies.

i)    *Trend studies:* When the researcher needs to analyse a trend of a phenomenon in a population, they conduct trend studies. The sample of the selected population might not be the same (as over a period of time they might have shifted or not available for various reasons) but they belong to the same population. This selected population is sampled and examined regularly. Since it is a type of longitudinal research, it may not be started as well as ended by just one researcher or research project. An example of trend studies may be a yearly survey of number of graduates actively using books and journals from the library of a university.

ii) *Cohort studies:* The focus of this type of longitudinal study is also on a particular population which is sampled and studied more than once within a time gap. For example, in a district, prior to introduction of in-service training of teachers through DIETs, teacher's reaction towards in-service education was studied.

iii) *Panel studies:* The researcher in a panel study uses the same sample of people every time and that sample is called as a 'panel'. Such a study is used in order to investigate the changes in attitudes, behaviour or practices of the same panel within a period of time. They are more specific and focused as the researcher studies a particular change in the attitude, behaviour, belief or practice of the same group. For example, attitude of a particular group of students towards school education is studied over a period of time. Sample respondents remain the same for different phases of study.

## 18. What are the different types of questions that can be designed for a Survey instrument?

Broadly survey questions can be divided as structured and unstructured questions.
Each one of them is explained below:

**A)** **Structured questions** are those questions, the format of which is pre-planned and predefined in advance. Some of the types of structured questions include

(i)        Dichotomous Questions. (ii) Level of measurement based questions (iii) Filter or Contingency Questions

i)        *Dichotomous questions*

A question is said to be dichotomous if it has only two possible responses (for example – yes or no/ true or false and so on). The layout of these questions appears in the following ways in the questionnaire:

Does the library of your university has an electronic data base system?

————Yes

————No

ii) *Level of measurement based questions*

Not to be mentioned that three basic levels of measurement are: nominal (based on names, classification of persons, objects and groups), ordinal (based on ranks and preferences) and interval (based on ratings) measurements. For example, a nominal question may have numbers before each response, which may only represent the serial order, like –

Please state the category to which you belong:
General- ——————-
OBC- ——————
SC/ST- ——————

The numbers here just denote the serial order and have nothing to do with the preference or ranks.

A question based on the ordinal level of measurement will be based on the preference or choice of the respondent. For example, the respondent may be asked to give a ranking for the business tycoons in an order of most trendy or fashionable to least trendy, where the respondent may be asked to give a rank of 1 to the most trendy tycoon and 4 to the least trendy tycoon:

——————————— Subroto Roy
——————————— Mukesh Ambani
——————————— Bill Gates
——————————— Vijay Mallya

The respondent may rank the tycoons on the basis of their own likings and preferences.
The question based on interval scale may be based on rating the choices, out of which the most commonly used scale is Likert response scale (which has a rating of 1 to5, or 1to7, or, 1 to 9).

iii) *Filter or Contingency Questions*
When a question is framed in such a way that it is followed by succeeding questions, which are sub

parts of the main question, such types of question design is known as filter or contingency questions.

For example, if a researcher wants to ask whether the respondent has ever attended the library of the university and if the researcher also wants to know how many times the respondent has attended the library, then the format of the question will be as follows:

Have you ever regularly attended the library of your university? **Survey Research**

Yes    No

If yes, then how many times?

Once in a month

Twice in a month

Every week of the month

Each and every day in a month

The researcher may use multiple filter questions in order to get the subsequent responses. But he or she should take full care that in order to maintain the interest of the respondent, they should not exceed more than two to three levels for any question.

B) **Unstructured questions** are usually used in interview, where either the researcher does not prepare a list of questions and the series of questions might depend upon the response of the subjects or they ask questions in an informal atmosphere. In order to get adequate and required information, the researcher should take full care and should give a silent probe, verbally encourage, ask for clarification and have full empathy with the respondent.

## 19. What are the advantages and disadvantages of Survey Research?

Survey research has the following advantages:
• It is convenient, less time taking and economical for the researcher.
• It is a versatile method, which can be applied to almost all types of research, including market research, political research, psychological and social research.
• It enables the analysis of data to be based on the laws of mathematics and statistics, arguably reducing the likelihood that ill-considered conclusions will be drawn from research.
• The survey can be conducted for a longer period of time, which gives a chance of knowing about the latest changes or advancements that might have taken place in the agenda under study
• The researcher gets a full chance to well organise and present the reasons of the study to get full and honest answers from the respondents.
• It is a cost-effective method for finding out about large populations.

**Disadvantages**
• Maintaining the privacy of responses of each respondent under a group interview is questionable and that may also restrict full and honest answers from them.
• High attrition rate of the respondents might hinder the longitudinal based studies.

## 20. Highlight the issues related to Survey Research?

If the researcher plans to go for a survey research, there are certain issues which he or she might have to understand and take full care. They are:

### 1) **Issues on selecting the type of Survey**
One of the most critical decisions for a researcher is to select the kind of survey that might be most appropriate or suitable for his or her study. The researcher should be aware of the kind of population that would be suitable for the study. Again, they should also be comfortable with the language of the selected population. The researcher should also analyse the geographic restrictions and try to find out which method can be most feasible for a dispersed population.

### 2) **Issues on survey instruments Survey Research**
While constructing the survey, the researcher should have full knowledge of the suitability of the questions that would be asked to the respondents. The type of questions, clarity and specificity of the questions as well as the length of the questions are some of the controversial issues within a survey research.

### 3) **Bias Issues**
The researcher's bias and prejudices might have a significant influence on the findings of the survey research, so they should be fully aware of the repercussions of their bias. Their behaviour should be socially desired ones, he or she should not lose track and also should avoid false reports. In such cases,

issues of bias are really difficult but essential agenda in a survey research.

## 4) **Administrative Issues**

The cost, mode of survey, feasibility of the area selected, required time period are also important aspects which needs to be pre-planned even before the advancement of the research.

## 21. Discuss the concept of Ex-Post Facto Research?

The term ex-post facto according to Landman (1988: 62) is used to refer to an experiment in which a researcher, instead of finding a treatment, examines the effect of a naturally occurring treatment after it has occurred. In other words it is a study that attempts to discover the pre-existing causal conditions between groups.

The ex-post facto research is a kind of research in which the researcher predicts the possible causes behind an effect that has already occurred.

For example, if a child is delinquent (that is, one who indulges in criminal activities), then in order to find the basic reason behind such delinquency, the researcher would try to find out the various events that have occurred and the many possibilities that could have contributed to the concerned delinquent behaviour. The expected possibilities may be lack of discipline at school/ family history/ peer effect/ neighbourhood or socialisation.

It is an interesting point to note that, the researcher predicts a cause on the basis of a controlled effect (since no variation can be done on the effect which has already taken place on the basis of the independent variable or the cause).

## *CHARACTERISTICS OF EX POST FACTO RESEARCH*

Based on the concept of the ex-post factor research, it is also known as 'causal comparative research'.
The ex-post facto research has certain characteristic which distinguishes it from other different types of researches.

### The research has a control or a comparison group
As the research is done on basis of the study of the cause which has already led to its effects, it becomes necessary for the researcher to keep a control group, which can be used for comparison with the actual experimental group later on? in order to analyse the cause of an already occurred event.

### The behaviour, action, event or the treatment or the independent variable of the research cannot be manipulated or changed
As the ex-post research is a kind of study which tries to predict the causes on the basis of actions that have already occurred, the researcher cannot manipulate or change the already occurred actions or behaviour.

### The research focuses on the effects
Since the researcher tries to analyse and predict the reasons behind the occurrence of an event or

phenomena, their first attempt is to focus on the event or the phenomena that has already occurred. Only after having a detailed study of the phenomena or the event, the researcher tries to determine the causes behind such an event or phenomena.

**The research tries to analyse the 'how' and 'what' aspect of an event**
Since the researcher tries to understand the causal effects behind a phenomena, the research basically focuses on how and what reasons that has led that phenomena to occur.

**Explores possible effects and causes**
With the help of an ex-post facto research, the researcher tries to analyse the cause and effect phenomena of an event, action or behaviour.

## 22. What are the steps included in ex-post facto research?

The process of ex-post facto research is systematic and follows a definite sequence. As mentioned by Isaac and Michael (1971), the following are the steps involved in the expost facto research—

**Step 1. Determining the problem**
In an ex-post facto research, it is necessary for the researcher to focus on the problem that he or she needs to study. They not only need to find out a problem, they also need to determine, analyse and define the problem which they will be dealing with.

## Step 2. Literature Review

Before trying to predict the causal relationships, the researcher needs to study all the related or similar literature and relevant studies, which may help in further analysis, prediction and conclusion of the causal relationship between the variables under study.

## Step 3. Formulation of hypothesis

The third step of the ex-post facto research is to propose the possible solutions or alternatives that might have led to the effect. They need to list out the assumptions which will be the basis of the hypothesis and procedure of the research.

## Step 4. Designing the approach

Once the problem has been defined and the hypothesis has been postulated, the researcher needs to select the sample which fits the criteria of the study. They also need to select the scale or construct instrument for collecting the required information / data. Once the designing are all finalised, the researcher analyses the relationship between the variables.

## Step 5. Validity of the research

The researcher needs to validate the significance of their research. They need to be cautious regarding the extent to which their findings would be valid and significant and helpful in interpreting and drawing inferences from the obtained results.

## Step 6. Interpretation of the conclusion

Finally, the researcher needs to analyse, evaluate and interpret the information collected. It is on basis of this step only, the researcher selects the best possible alternative of causes which might have led the effect to occur.

Similarly, Jacobs et al. (1992: 81) also proposed that the following steps are involved in conducting an ex-post facto-research:

1st Step: The first step should be to state the problem.

2nd Step: Following this is the determination of the group to be investigated. Two groups of the population that differ with regard to the variable should be selected in a proportional manner for the test sample.

3rd step: The next step refers to the process of collection of data. Techniques like questionnaires, interviews, literature search etc. are used to collect the relevant information.

4th Step: The last step is the interpretation of the findings and the results. Based on the conclusions the hypothesis is either accepted or rejected.

It must be remembered that even though the ex-post facto research is a valid method for collecting information regarding an event that had already occurred, this type of research has shortcomings, and that only partial control is possible.

## 23. Differentiate between an Experimental and ex-post facto research?

| | Experimental research | Ex-post facto research |
|---|---|---|
| Control over independent Variable | In an experimental research, the researcher can directly manipulate the independent variable/s (that is, the cause) in order to examine its effect on the dependent variable (that is, the effect). | In an ex-post facto research, the researcher can not directly manipulate the independent variable/s (that is, the cause) as he or she predicts the cause on basis of the dependent variable (that is, the effect). |
| Principle of randomisation | The researcher can use the principle of randomisation in an experimental research on basis of which they can conclude or infer that other things remaining equal/constant/controlled the effect is a result of manipulation of the cause. | The researcher can not use the principle of randomisation in an ex-post facto research as the researcher has no direct control over the cause and so they infer the possibilities of the causes on basis of the existing effect. |
| Manipulation of variables | The researcher can manipulate variables in an experimental research | The researcher can not manipulate variables in an ex-post facto research. |
| Interpretation | It is easier to interpret or infer relationships between the independent and dependent variables as they can manipulate the independent variable and see its effect on dependent variable | It is difficult to interpret or infer relationship between the independent and dependent variables as there can be more than one possibilities or cause for a particular effect. |

## 24. What is meant by Experimental Research and identify its features?

Experimental research is the description and analysis of what will be, or what will occur, under carefully controlled conditions. It provides a method of hypothesis testing. Hypothesis is the heart of experimental research.

Experimental research is mainly used in science subjects such as physics, chemistry, medicine, biology etc.

Experiment requires two variables, one independent variable and the other dependent variable. It is important that in experimental research the independent variable is manipulated and the effect of manipulation is observed on the dependent variable.

All other extraneous factors are completely controlled within the laboratory. It is based on research design which uses manipulation and controlled testing to understand the causal processes.

Generally, we can manipulate one or more variables to determine their effect on a dependent variable. In other words it is a systematic and scientific approach to research in which the researcher manipulates one or more variables, and controls and measures the other variables.

Four essential characteristics of Experimental research:

a)  Control
b)  Manipulation
c)  Observation
d)  Replication

Control refers to removing or minimising the influence of extraneous variables which are not of direct interest to researcher, by means of methods like ANCOVA [Application of statistical technique of analysis of Covariance].

Manipulation refers to a deliberate operation of the independent variable on the subjects of the experimental group by the researcher to observe its effect. In this process, a pre-determined set of conditions called Independent / experimental variable which is also treatment variable.

E.g. Sex, socio-economic status, intelligence, method of teaching, training or qualification of teacher and classroom environment are major independent variables in educational research.

In Observation, experimenter observes the effect of the manipulation of the independent variable on dependent variable. E.g. performance or achievement in a task.

Replication is a matter of conducting a number of sub-experiments, instead of one experiment only, within the framework of same experimental design.

## 25. Discuss the strength and weakness of Field experiment?

Field experiments on the other hand refer to experiments conducted in real life situations. Here the control of extraneous factors is not possible as it is a natural setting and there is no way to control any factor as absolutely as one does in the laboratory experiments. Hence in field experiments we take two groups matched for a number of factors such as age, sex, education, socio-economic status etc.

Both these groups are in real life setting and thus are subjected to similar extraneous variables and thus the experimenter can observe the effects of his manipulation on one group and compare with the other group which is not subjected to any intervention.

Take for example that the researcher wants to study the effects of different methods of teaching (e.g. lecture vs. tutorial). The school is the natural setting from where the researcher randomly selects 100 children from a particular standard (5th standard) and randomly assign them to two groups, viz., experimental (50 children) and control group (50 children).

To the experimental group children the researcher uses the lecture method and to the control group tutorial method. Then the effects of the academic performance of these children are compared before and after the introduction of the methods of teaching. If there is a difference in the academic performance of children in regard to the two methods of teaching, the experimenter can conclude that a particular method of teaching (e.g. tutorial) is more effective than the other method (lecture).

The advantages or the strength of field experiments are given below:

a)  It is useful to behavioural and social scientists such as the social psychologists, sociologists and educationists.
b)  It is an appropriate method for studying complex social influences, processes, and changes in life like setting. The dynamics and small groups have been fruitfully studied by this method.
c)  It is most suited method to the testing of theory and to the solution of practical problems.
d)  It is suited to testing broad hypotheses.
e)  Flexibility and applicability to a wide variety of problems are also possible by this method.

Weaknesses or limitations of field experiments are as given below:

a)  The chances of extraneous variables confounding the research findings are more in field experiments due to the uncontrolled extraneous variables.
b)  One of the problems is the negative attitude of researcher.
c)  Consent and cooperation of concerned subjects and the institutional authorities, (the

institution where the research is to be conducted) is required for the field experiment.

d) This type of research faces lack of precision problem.

## 26. What are the steps through which field experiment is conducted?

Before constructing an experiment research there are various aspects to consider.

a) *Planning:* A good planning always ensures that the research is carried out properly and in proper conditions with appropriate tools and measures.

b) *Sampling*: One of the best ways to ensure that the research is conducted systematically and appropriately is to have a proper selection of sample.

**Sampling** is taking any portion of a population or universe as representative of that population or universe. Sample can be classified into *probability* and *non-probability sample.*

Probability samples use some form of random sampling in one or more of their stages. Non probability samples do not use random sampling; they thus lack the virtues being discussed. Still, they are often necessary and unavoidable.

The probability sampling includes stratified, cluster, systematic and random sampling method.

The non-probability sampling includes quota, purposive and accidental sampling method.

c) *Research design*: Every research requires a blue print of the research work that will be carried out. Where the experiment will be conducted, that is the setting, who will be the subjects, that is the sample, how it will be conducted, what instruments will be used, what will be manipulated, what will be measured etc. The experimental design must also provide for the number of subjects that will be in the experiment and the number of subjects who will be considered as the control group.

d) *Tools of data collection*: What are the tools that will be used, how the results will be measured, and what statistical tools will be used etc?

e) *Procedure*: Once the subjects have been identified and setting has been decided where the experiment will be conducted, the next step is to get permission from authorities to use the setting. Having obtained the permission let us say from school authorities to conduct field experiment regarding which method of teaching leads to better academic performance, the subjects will be selected from a certain class.

Let us say we choose children from class 5 all sections. Let us say there are 200 children. We need only 100 children and so from each of the 4 sections we take 25 out of 50 children randomly. From these 100 children, we again take 50 for control group and another 50 for experiment. This again we select randomly. Both the groups children are tested for academic performance and their scores are recorded. Then, to the experimental group of children we give instruction through lecture method and to the other group through tutorial method.

After training for 1 month, the academic performances of both the groups are retested. Now the difference in the second testing for the two groups will indicate which method is more effective. Within the group also the pre and the post-test performance could be measured and the difference noted as improvement or decrease in academic performance.

6) _Statistical analysis_: Appropriate statistics such as the t test will be used to find if the differences obtained between the two groups as well as between the pre and the post tests are statistically significant.

## 27. Outline the differences between Experimental research and Field experiments?

There are considerable differences between the experimental research and field experiments which are given in the table below:

| Experimental research | Field experiment |
|---|---|
| 1) The subjects are homogeneous. | 1) The subjects may vary in a number of characteristics. |
| 2) The experimental subjects are in controlled conditions. | 2) The subjects are not in controlled but in natural settings and conditions. |
| 3) One experimental group is taken and subjected to the manipulation of the independent variable (Intervention) and see the effects of it on the subjects of the experimental group. | 3) Two groups matched for certain basic characteristics which may confound the results are taken and one is subjected to intervention while the other is not. At the end the results of two groups on a dependent variable are compared to see the effect of intervention. |
| 4) The cause effect relationship can be clearly established as in the laboratory experiment all extraneous factors are controlled and the pure effects of intervention can be studied. | 4) The cause effect relationship can be established to quite an extent but not to the same accuracy of experimental research as extraneous factors are not controlled as in the laboratory. |
| 5) Predication based on the experiment is possible and one can even accurately predict a phenomenon given the same conditions. | 5) Prediction is possible to certain extent as the real life situation may not be the same in all places where the study is conducted. |
| 6) The experiment is always quantitative in terms of results. | 6) The field experiment is both qualitative and quantitative in terms of results. |
| 7) The experiment is replicable. | 7) The field experiments are replicable but may require modifications in terms of the matching factors. |

## 28. Explain the basic objectives of Research design?

A Research design is the arrangement of conditions for collection and analysis of data in a manner that aims to combine relevance to the research purpose with economy in procedure.

Research can be explained as Re + Search= again + explore, to explore the relationship between different variables.

Research is a scientific methodology in a controlled setting. Observation and experiments are the basic scientific tools of research which gives the scientific status to the field of psychology.

The controlled observation means that we have to see the impact of independent variable and dependent variable under specific controlled condition and we have to manipulate the independent variable in a systematic way and record the relative changes in the dependent variable.

For controlled observation it is essential for one to manipulate independent variables with certain controls and the principles of randomisation should be followed. In other words a good research design is that in which we can forecast or give a solution to the problem.

According to Kerlinger (1998), Research design is the
i) *plan,*
ii) *structure, and*
iii) *strategy* of investigation.

The research design is conceived so as to obtain answers to research questions and to control variance. The above three aspects of research design are being explained below:

i)     Plan is the overall scheme or programme of the study. It can be in the form of proposal of the study.

ii)     Structure of the research is more specific. It is the outline, the scheme, the paradigm of the operation of the variables.

iii)     Strategy is more specific than plan. The method that we want to use to collect the data and analyse or interpret the data. The strategy also implies as to how the research objectives will be reached and how the problems encountered in the research will be tackled.

According to Myers (1980), the design is the general structure of the experiments, not its specific content.

**<u>Objectives of Research Design</u>:**

The research design has two basic objectives:

i)     **To provide answers to research questions** – The investigator has the answer to research questions in the form of validity, objectivity, accuracy and economical aspects of the research concerned. The researcher is not inclined to answer the research questions in a layman's term but answer in terms of validity, objectivity, accuracy etc. For example, the factorial design is a design which deals with the interaction effect in an economical way. Different research problems require different research designs.

Research problems can be and are stated in the form of hypotheses and the research designs are carefully worked out to yield dependent and valid answers to the research questions epitomised by the hypotheses. If the hypothesis discussed is one of interaction, a factorial design is evidently more appropriate (Analysis of variance is used in factorial design).

The adequate planning and executed design helps to make efficient observation and draw appropriate inferences from the result.

An adequate research design would suggest the number of observations that have to be made, and which variables are active and which are attributed Etc. According to the adequate research design we can then act to manipulate the active variables and to categorize the attribute variables.

ii)    **To control variance under study–** The score deviation is called variance and these variances must be controlled. The investigators follow certain principles for constructing an efficient research design.

*Principle 1: To maximise the variance of variable*

The main concern of the investigators is to maximise the variance in a systematic way. It is called the *experimental variance.*

The Variance of the dependent variable (DV) is influenced by the independent variable (IV). The main task of an experimenter is to maximise the variance.

If the independent variable does not vary substantially, there is little chance of separating its effect from the total variance of the dependent variable.

Hence it is necessary to give chance to the variance to show itself separately from the total variance. The purpose of a good research design is to maximise systematic variance.

Principle 2: *To control extraneous variance*
The purpose of the effective research design is to control extraneous variance which may confound the results of the experiment.

There are three ways to control extraneous variables confounding the results:
i) to eliminate the variable as a variable;
ii) to control extraneous variance through randomisation,
iii) to build it right into the design as an independent variable.

Principle 3: *To minimise error variance*
Our aim is to minimise error variance from the research study. It is unpredictable.

Some time we see the impact of constant error in the study.
*For example,* individual differences and intelligence. This type of error affects adversely the research findings.

We can minimise the error variance by two basic methods:
i) the reduction of errors of measurement through controlled conditions and
ii) an increase in the reliability of measures.

## 29. Discuss critically the three types of Experimental Research Design?

The pure experimental research is not always possible in behavioural and social sciences due to the difficulty in controlling all the variables and influences from outside of and inside the individuals who is possible only within a laboratory situation.

The experimental situations in which experimenter can manipulate the independent variables and has liberty to assign subjects randomly to the treatment groups and the control groups may not be that possible or accurate.

Also the control of the extraneous variables is not possible and children in a classroom keep getting stimulation from various sources. Hence one has to take such designs in which to the extent possible randomisation and control of variances are possible.

To conduct the field experiments there are experimental designs available and these are being discussed below.

### A)  *Single Case Experimental Design*

The single case experiment is useful in clinical research especially in the area of behaviour modification. This design provides us the detailed information of human behaviour which is not possible in the group designs. Repeated measurements are also possible and we can note subtle changes in the subjects' behaviour.

The design however is not very suitable for generalising the findings to the larger population as it is based on a small number of subjects and who have not been randomly selected.

### B)  *Quasi-Experimental Design*

All experimental situations in which the researcher / experimenter do not have full control over the assignment of experimental units randomly to the treatment conditions or the treatment cannot be manipulated, are collectively called quasi experimental designs.

There are the various experimental situations in which the experimenter does not have full control over the situations. The plan of such experiments constitutes the quasi- experimental design.

Though, quasi-experimental investigations have limitations, nevertheless these have advantages in certain respects. It is possible to select subjects randomly as pointed out earlier in the case of selecting students from class 5 of a school and randomly assign them to the experimental and control groups respectively. We conduct the experiment in natural and real life setting and so it has certain amount of realism and the information so gathered can also be to quite an extent generalised. It can provide answers to several kinds of problems about past situations and those situations which cannot be handled by employing pure experimental research design.

### C) *Experimental Design*

This type of design is generally conducted in the laboratory with complete control over all variables and all subjects. In this type of research design one can assign subjects randomly to the treatment groups and one can manipulate the independent variable and study the pure effects of the manipulation on the dependent variable.

Also, in such experiments, the experimenter has complete control over the scheduling of independent variables. In such experiments one can use high level advanced statistical methods got analyse the data.

For example, the $F$ test, Correlation and regression and multiple regression analysis, partial correlation etc.

There are also three types of designs that we can use within the experimental design and these are
    (i)      Between subjects design

(ii)     (ii) Within subject design and
(iii)    Mixed design
(iv)     classical pre-test post-test design
(v)      Solomon four groups design
(vi)     Factorial design.


i)    *Between subject design* – Each subject is observed only under one of the several treatments conditions.

ii)   *Within subject deign or repeated measures design* – Each subject is observed under all the treatment conditions involved in the experiment.

iii)  *Mixed design* – Some factors are involved from between subjects and some are from within subjects.

iv)   *Classical pre-test-post-test* – The total population of participants is randomly divided into two samples; the control sample, and the experimental sample.

Only the experimental sample is exposed to the manipulated variable. The researcher compares the pre-test results with the post test results for both samples Any divergence in the results between the two samples is assumed to be a result of the experiment.

v)    *Solomon four group design* – The sample is randomly divided into four groups. Two of the groups are experimental samples. Two groups experience no experimental manipulation of variables. Two groups receive a pre-test and a post test. Two groups receive only a post test. This is an improvement over the classical design because it controls for the effect of the pre-test.

vi)    *Factorial design* – This is similar to a classical design except additional samples are used. Each group is exposed to a different experimental manipulation.

All the above designs of research can be used in experimental research work for analysing the data. On the other hand these designs are not suitable for conducting field experiments though one could use them with certain modifications.

## 30. Write a brief note on Case Study?

Case study provides a systematic and scientific way of perceiving or examining events, collect data, analyse information, and prepare a report.

In other words, case study should be defined as a research strategy, an empirical inquiry that investigates a phenomenon within its real-life context.

Case study research means single and multiple case studies, can include quantitative evidence, relies on multiple sources of evidence and benefits from the prior development of theoretical propositions. Case studies based on any evidence of quantitative and qualitative research.

Single subject-research provides the statistical framework for making inferences from quantitative case-study data.

According to Lamnek (2005) "The case study is a research approach, situated between concrete data taking techniques and methodologic paradigms."

Psychoanalyst Sigmund Freud used case study method to assist his subjects in solving personality problems. The detailed accounts of interviews with subjects and his interpretations of their thoughts, dreams and action provide excellent examples of case studies.

Guidance counsellors, social workers and other practitioners conduct case studies for diagnosing particular condition or problem and recommending remedial measures. They collect data from a particular individual and confine their interest to the individual as a unique case or collect data from a small group of individuals, which form a unit for depth study.

**Criteria for Selection of Case Study:**

For selection of cases for the case study, we often use information oriented sampling. Our cases are based on this only information, which is mostly based on the extreme cases or typical cases.

Random samples emphasising representativeness will seldom be able to produce this kind of insight. It is more appropriate to select a few cases for their validity, but this is not always the case. Three types of information oriented cases may be distinguished:

- Critical cases
- Extreme or deviant cases
- Paradigmatic cases

Yin (2005) suggested that researchers should decide whether to do single-case or multiple-case studies and choose to keep the case holistic or have embedded sub-cases.

**Types of Case Studies**:

There are four types of case studies which are (i) illustrative case studies (ii) exploratory case studies (iii) cumulative case studies and (iv) critical instance case studies.

1) **Illustrative Case Studies:** These are primarily descriptive studies. They typically utilise one or two instances of an event to show what a situation is like. Illustrative case studies serve primarily to make the unfamiliar familiar and to give readers a common language about the topic in question.

2) **Exploratory (or pilot) Case Studies:** This type of case studies performed before implementing a large scale investigation. Their basic function is to help identify questions and select types of measurement prior to the main investigation. The primary pit fall of this type of study is that initial findings may seem

convincing enough to be released prematurely as conclusions.

3) **Cumulative Case Studies:** These serve to aggregate information from several sites collected at different times. The idea behind these studies is the collection of past studies will allow for greater generalisation without additional cost or time being expended on new, possibly repetitive studies.

4) **Critical Instance Case Studies:** These examine one or more sites for either the purpose of examining a situation of unique interest with little to no interest in generalisability, or to call into question or challenge a highly generalised or universal assertion. This method is useful for answering cause and effect questions.

**Steps for Case Study**:

The following steps are used in the conduct of a case study:

**Step 1. Determining the present status of the case or cases**

The first step is to determine the present status of the case or cases through direct observation. In addition to physical examination of the case or cases, a psychological evaluation is required to determine the general ability level etc.

For example, to make a case study of a 'slow learner', the first thing to do is to determine the present status of the child by making an assessment of his physique cognitive factors through direct observation and psychological test.

## Step 2. Identifying the most probable antecedents of the case or cases

Determining the most probable antecedents of the case or cases is the next important steps. This information helps in formulating a workable hypothesis or a set of hypothesis. For example, in case of 'slow learner' cited in Step 1, the researcher may formulate a hypothesis that occurrence of slow learning behaviour in the child is due to unhealthy have environment, bad study habits and poor teaching in the school.

## Step 3. Verification of Antecedents/Hypotheses

The case is then checked for the presence or absence of the antecedents supposed to apply to situation of under study.

For example, the behaviour of slow learning of the child. This involves multi-method approach, which includes observation, past history of the case, interview etc.

## Step 4. Diagnosis and Remedial Measures

After the verification of the antecedents or hypothesis (es , the next step is directed towards the diagnosis of the causes (example, causes of slow learning) and suggesting remedial measures in the light of the causes.

## Step 5. Follow-up of the case or cases

The last step of the case study is the follow-up of the case (es) to study the impact of remedial measures. If impact is positive, the diagnosis is taken to be correct.

**Ways of Case Studies**:

There are different ways of using case studies, which are given below:

### 1) Writing analysis of case study

The most careful analysis of a case study is probably obtained when it is made in writing. Case studies can be used as term papers with other related readings and bibliographies.

### 2) Panel of experts

Although group members miss the advantages of participation, listening to a panel of experts a case may be useful especially as an introduction to the case method. A variation of this technique would be to bring in a panel of experts to analyse a case after a group had already done so.

### 3) Analysis of similar case studies Case Study

Another variation of case discussion is to collect from the group members incidents from their experience similar to the case under consideration.
Generalisations drawn from the case under consideration may carry over to the experiences of other members.

**4) Cross examination**

By cross examination group members with questions prepared in advance, they will discover that it is necessary to do careful thinking and preparation before entering into case study. This technique, especially appropriate for use with cases containing a great deal of detail, gives the researcher many opportunities to ask individuals to defend their points of views in terms of the data presented.

## 31. Discuss the meaning and function of Research Design?

Research design is the plan, structure and strategy of investigation conceived so as to obtain answers to research questions and to control variance. The plan is the overall scheme or the program of the research. It includes an outline of what the investigator will do from writing the hypothesis and their operational implications to the final analysis of data.

Structure of the research is outline of the research design, and the scheme is the paradigm of operation of the variable.

Strategy includes the methods to be used to gather and analyse the data. In other words, strategy implies how the research objective will be reached and how the problems encountered in the research will be tackled. (Kerlinger, 2007).
A traditional research design is a blueprint or detailed plan as to how a research study is to be completed. That is, how it would operationalise variables so that

they can be measured, how to select a sample of interest to the research topic, how to collect data to be used as a basis for testing hypothesis, and how to analyse the results. (Thyer, 1993).

It is essential to get familiar with some term for clear and better understanding of the design.

### i) **Factors Single Factor Design**

The independent variable of an experiment is known as factor of the experiment. An experiment always has at least one factor.

### ii) **Levels**

A level is a particular value of an independent variable. An independent variable has at least two levels. For example if we are intended to see the effect of reward on verbal learning. Then reward is the factor and it has two levels, reward or no reward.

### iii) **Treatment**

It refers to a particular set of experimental condition. For example in 2 × 2 factorial experiment the subject are assigned to 4 treatments.

The Function of Research Design is
- (i) to provide answer to research question and
- (ii) to enable the researcher to answer research question as validly, accurately and as economically as possible.

According to Kerlinger (2007), the research design has two basic purposes,

(i)     to provide answer to research question and

(ii)    to control variance. In other words, the purpose of research design is to get dependable and valid answers to research questions.

(iii)   Research problems are stated in the form of hypothesis. The research design guides the researcher how to collect data for testing the formulated hypothesis.

*The main function of research design is to control variance. The statistical principle behind this mechanism is MAXMINCON principle, that is, Maximise systematic variance, Control extraneous variance and Minimise error variance. (Kerlinger, 2007).*

Systematic variance is the variability in the dependent measure due to the manipulation of the independent variable. In addition to independent and dependent variables, there are other variables that may influence dependent variable known as extraneous variable. Different methods are used to control the extraneous variable and some of these methods are for example, randomisation, elimination and matching. The term error variance means that variance which occurs due to the variables that are not controllable by the experimenter.

**32. What do you understand the following Single Factor Designs?**
**A) Between Group Design and**
**B) Within Subject Design**

**A)** **Between Group Design:**

This is a way of avoiding the carryover effects that can plague with-in subjects designs and they are one of the most common experiment types in some scientific disciplines, especially Psychology.

Here subjects are assigned at random to different treatment conditions. Here the effect of different conditions on the subjects are computed. In this you can have
(i) two randomised group design or (ii) Multigroup design.

As for the two randomised group design , in this we randomly assign the subjects into two groups. For this type of design, the experimenter first defines the independent variable, dependent variable and the research population. For example an investigator wants to see the effect of knowledge of result on the rate of learning of school students in a particular city. Researcher randomly selects a sample of 100 students from a city. Then researcher will randomly divide these 100 students in two groups with 50 students in experimental group and 50 students in control group. The random assignment of the subjects into two groups can be done by various methods.

The most common method of randomly assigning the subjects into two groups is to use the table of random number. To divide the subjects into experimental and control group, the researcher may write down the name of all the students in alphabetical order on a paper and assign 1st student in experimental group, the 2nd in control group, 3rd in experimental group and so on. The researcher also may write the name of the subjects on separate slips fold them and place them in a box and pick the slip one by one. The experimenter may place first slip in one group and second in the second group. It is expected that these two groups will not differ significantly at the start of the experiment.

Now the students of experimental group will receive the knowledge of result of their performance and the students of control group do not receive the feedback of their performance.
Then the scores of all subjects of experimental and control group will be recorded and subjected to statistical analysis. If the statistical test reveals that two groups differ significantly on dependent variable then it can be concluded that the difference in rate of learning is due to the manipulation of independent variable.

If the rate of learning of experimental group is more than that of the control group, then we may conclude that knowledge of result facilitated the learning.

In two randomised group design 't' test or Mann-Whitney U test is most commonly applied statistical techniques design.

### _More than two randomised group design or multi group design_

In behavioural science, the researcher sometimes uses more than two randomised group design. In such studies, there are more than two or three experimental groups and one control group.

For example in an educational experiment, let us say that we want to study the effect of schedule of reinforcement on the rate of learning of a verbal task. We have three experimental groups and one control group. The experimental group ($G_1$) receives reinforcement of every response , while the experimental group 2 ($G_2$) receives reinforcement at regular time interval, and the third experimental group ($G_3$) receives reinforcement at random interval and the control group ($G_4$) receives no reinforcement. We measure the rate of learning on the verbal tasks of all these groups and use statistical technique to answer research question.

In more than two randomised group design some time we have three or four experimental groups only.

For example an experimenter wants to study the effect of four teaching methods on learning of a particular task. Suppose for this, the **Single Factor Design** researcher randomly selects 100 students and assign 25 subject randomly in each group. These groups are supposed to be equivalent groups after random assignment. In the experiment, one group will be taught by method A, the second by method B, third by method C and fourth by method D. All subjects were administered a particular task and the scores are obtained on dependent variable. Through appropriate statistical technique we can find out which method of teaching is most effective. In multi group design the two most commonly applied statistic is the one way analysis of variance and Duncan Range test.

### *Matched group design*

This design is also known as randomised block design (Edwards, 1968).

In matched group design all subjects are first tested on a common task and then they are formed into groups. The groups thus formed are known as equivalent groups. Subsequently, the different values of the independent variable are introduced to each group and the mean scores of the dependent variable are taken of both the groups. The matching variable is usually different from the variable under study but is, in general related to it. The two groups are not necessarily of the same size although there should not be large differences in the number of subjects of two groups.

When we use the matched group design the most important factor is the identification of the variables on which matching has to be done. The matching variable should have high correlation with dependent variable. Sometime the dependent variable itself is used as matching variable.

Sometime an independent measure may be used as matching variable. But the variable selected should be somewhat related to the dependent variable. For example in a study the researcher wants to see the effect of praise on subject's performance on intelligence test.

We have two groups, one group is praised for its performance on the test and urged to try to better its scores and the second group does not receive any comment. For assigning the subjects into two groups the researcher may find the scores on form A of the intelligence test and obtained the set of scores. On the basis of the obtained scores on form A subjects can be paired off. Those subjects who scored 100 were selected for the study. They were divided into two groups randomly and form B of the same test was administered to see the effect of incentive on subject's score. Suitable statistical test is used to find-out the significant difference in the mean scores of two groups.

In matched group design we may use two methods of matching.

*Matching by pairs*
In this type of research, matching is done initially by pairs so that each person in the first group has a match in the second group. For example researcher wants to study the effect of two teaching methods on mathematical achievement of the IX grade students. Subjects Intelligence and academic achievement was taken as matching variable. All subjects were administered mathematical academic achievement test and scores were obtained. If for instance two subjects scored 80, then one subject is placed in one group and another is placed in another group. In this way two groups are formed. One group is taught by

one method and another group is taught by another method and academic achievement scores of both the groups are compared.

*Matching in terms of mean and SD*
When it is impractical or impossible to set up groups in which subjects have been matched person to person, investigators often resort to matching of groups in terms of Mean and Standard Deviation. The matching variable is somewhat related to the dependent variable. For example intelligence is a matching variable and the researcher obtained the mean and SD of intelligence scores of two groups.
In the matched group design the subject may be matched on age, educational level, learning ability and so on. However one should be very careful in choosing the matching variables.

## B) **Within Subject Design**:

Within subject design is also known as repeated measure design, because the same individual is treated differently at different times and we compare their scores after they have been subjected to different treatment conditions. For example, let us say a researcher wants to study the effect of colours on reaction time. The investigator selects three colours say red, green and yellow and let us say that 10 subjects are selected for the experiment from the population of interest.

After exposing them to different colours, their reaction time is noted and compared.

Within subject design is further divided into two categories, viz.,
(i)      Two conditions within subject design and
(ii)     Multiple condition within subject design.

### • _Two conditions, within subject design_
The two conditions design is the simplest design. The two conditions are labelled as 'condition 1' and 'condition 2'. All subjects experience both the conditions.

Let us say that the researcher wants to compare the reaction time of red and green colour. We select 10 subjects from the population of interest, and the reaction time of all the subjects is noted down for the two colours. Despite its simplicity, this design is not used as often as one might expect because many experimenters involve more than two conditions and there is possibility of carryover effect from one condition to the other.

### • _Multiple Conditions within subject design_
Psychology experiments generally employ more than two conditions. Usually the researcher wants to compare several variables or treatments and ascertain their effectiveness. Another reason for conducting multiple conditions experiment is to determine the shape of the function that relates the independent and dependent variables.

For example a researcher may want to know how the sensation of brightness increases with the physiological intensity of a light. For this the researcher may present each of several intensities of the light to a group of subjects.

From the responses to the various intensities, the researcher can plot the relation between intensity and brightness. This design can be explained by an example.

Fergus, Craik and Endel Tuluing (1975) examined whether different strategies of processing words would affect memory. They used different strategies for processing the word. They flashed words on a screen. Before each word appeared they asked the subject a question, "Is the word in capital letters?" or "Does the word rhyme with train ?" or "Does the word fit in this sense ?" The first strategy focused on the visual properties of the word, the second on the acoustic properties and the third on the semantic properties. Researcher hypothesised that each successive type of strategy would induce greater "depth of processing". Their theory predicted that increasing the depth of processing, would increase the memory for that word.

- ***Comparison between group and within subject design***

In the within subject design each subject in the experiment receives a number of treatments or conditions whereas in the 'between subject' design, a subject receives only one treatment.

In within subject design the experimenter repeats the measures on the same group of subject and this increases the precision of the experiment by eliminating intersubjective differences as a source of error.

Whether we will use the between group design or within subject design depends on the experimental situation. When there are chances of practice or carry over

## 33. What do you understand by Factorial Design with example?

A factorial design is one in which two or more variable or factors are employed in such a way that all the possible combinations of selected values of each variable are used (Mcburney & White, 2007).

According to Singh (1998), Factorial design is a design in which selected values of two or more independent variables are manipulated in all possible combinations so that their independent as well as interactive effect upon the dependent variable may be studied.

**Terms related to Factorial Design:**

**Factors:** The term factor is broadly used to include the independent variable that is manipulated by the investigator in the experiment or that is manipulated through selection. In the research some time it is possible to manipulate the independent variable directly, for example in a study researcher wants to study the effect of different drugs on the recovery of the patient. The researcher may select three dosages

2 mg, 4 mg. and 6 mg. and administer the drug to the subjects.

Further researcher may find that age is another important variable that may influence the rate of recovery from the diseases. The second independent variable that is age cannot be directly manipulated by the researcher. The manipulation of the variable 'age' is achieved through selection of the sample. The researcher then may divide the subjects into three age groups.

**Main Effect:** This is the simplest effect of a factor on a dependent variable. It is the effect of the factor alone averaged across the level of other factors.

According to Mcburney & White (2007) main effect in a factorial experiment, the effect of one independent variable, averaged over all levels of another independent variable.

**Interaction :** The conclusion based on the main effects of two independent variables may be at times misleading, unless we take into consideration the interaction effect of the two variables also.

According to Mcburney & White (2007) Interaction means when the effect of one independent variable depends on the level of another independent variable.

An interaction is the variation among the difference between mean for different levels of one factor over different levels of the other factor. For example a cholesterol reduction clinic has two diets and one exercise regime. It was found that exercise alone was effective and diet alone was effective in reducing cholesterol levels (main effect of exercise and main effect of diet).

## Types of Interaction

1) **Antagonistic interaction:** When main effect is non-significant and interaction is significant. In this situation the two independent variables tend to reverse each other's effect.

2) **Synergistic interaction:** When higher level of one independent variable enhances the effect of another independent variable.

3) **Celling effect interaction :** When the higher level of one independent variable reduces the differential effect of another variable. that is one variable has a smaller effect when paired with higher level of a second variable (Mcburney & White, 2007).

All of these types of interaction are common in psychological research.

**Randomisation:** Randomisation is the process by which experimental units are allocated to treatment; that is by a random process and not by any subjective process. The treatment should be allocated to units in such a way that each treatment is equally likely to be applied to each unit.

**Blocking:** This is the procedure by which experimental units are grouped into homogenous cluster in an attempt to improve the comparison of treatment by randomly allocating the treatment within each cluster or block.

In the two factor design we have two independent variables, each of which has two values or levels. This is known as two by two (2x2) factorial design because of the two levels of each variable.

## Layout of Factorial Design:

**2 × 2 Factorial Design**

| Factor B | Factor A | |
| --- | --- | --- |
| | $A_1$ | $A_2$ |
| $B_1$ | $A_1B_1$ | $A_2B_1$ |
| $B_2$ | $A_1B_2$ | $A_2B_2$ |

If we have two levels of one variable and three of another variable we would have two by three (2 × 3) factorial design.

**2 × 3 Factorial Design**

| Factors B | Factor A | | |
| --- | --- | --- | --- |
| | $A_1$ | $A_2$ | $A_3$ |
| $B_1$ | $A_1B_1$ | $A_2B_1$ | $A_3B_1$ |
| $B_2$ | $A_1B_2$ | $A_2B_2$ | $A_3B_2$ |

## Example of Factorial Design:

In an experiment Tulving and Pearlstone (1965) subjects were asked to learn a list of 12, 24 or 48 words (factor A with three levels). These words can be put in pairs by categories (for example apple and banana can be grouped as 'fruits').

Subjects were asked to learn these words and they were shown the category name at the same time as the words were presented. Subjects were told that they did not have to learn the category names. After a very short time, subjects were asked to recall the words. At that time half of the subjects were given the list of the category names, and the other half had to recall the words without the list of categories (factor B with two levels).

The dependent variable is the number of words recalled by each subjects is given in the table below:

Level of A

| Levels of B | $A_1$<br>12 words | $A_2$<br>24 words | $A_3$<br>48 words | Total |
|---|---|---|---|---|
| $B_1$<br>Cued recall | $A_1B_1$<br>(10) | $A_2B_1$<br>(13) | $A_3B_1$<br>(19) | 42 |
| $B_2$<br>Free recall | $A_1B_2$<br>(10) | $A_2B_2$<br>(15) | $A_3B_2$<br>(29) | 54 |
| Total | 20 | 28 | 48 | 96 |

Here we have two independent variables number of words and presence and absence of cues and one dependent variable that is the number of words recalled by each subject. We could do two separate experiments, one which varied the number of words and the other which varied the presence or absence of cues.

The first experiment could be as in Table 2. This table shows the independent effect of number of words. The second experiments could be as in Table 3.

**Table 2.2**

Cued Recall

| 12 Words | 24 Words | 48 Words |
|---|---|---|
| $A_1$ | $A_2$ | $A_3$ |

**Table 2.3**

Free recall

| 12 Words | 24 Words | 48 Words |
|---|---|---|
| $A_1$ | $A_2$ | $A_3$ |

In the above example (Table 2.1) there are six cells into which the sample is divided. Each of the six combinations would receive one treatment or experimental condition.

Subjects are assigned at random to each treatment in same manner as in a randomised group design. The mean (shown in bracket) for different cells may be obtained along with the means for different rows and columns. Means of different cells represent the mean scores for the dependent variable and the column mean in the given design are termed the main effect for number of words without taking into account any differential effect that is due to the presence or absence cues.

Similarly the row mean in the above design are termed the main effect for presence or absence of cues without regard to number of words. Thus through this design we can study not only the main effect of number of words and presence or absence of cues, but we can also study the interactive effect of number of words and presence or absence of cues, on the number of words recalled by the subject.

In this design we have two independent variables, we are able to examine two possible main effects. We found the main effect of number of words by averaging effect of number of words over the two levels of presence and absence of cues when we looked at the column mean. Similarly we found the main effect of presence or absence of categories by averaging the effect of presence or absence of categories over the three levels of number of words when we looked at the row mean.

By these results we can find out the interactive effect. Two variables interact if the effect of one variable depends on the level of the other. We have an interaction here. Because the effect of presence or absence of cues depends on the number of words. Similarly the retention is influence by the length of the test.

Interaction can be presented in a tabular form as well as in graphical form.

**Importance of Interaction**
Main effect is an average effect. It can be misleading when an interaction is present. When interaction is present we should examine the effect of any factor of interest at each level of the interacting factor before making interpretation (Minimum et.al. 2001). The two factor design is really made up of several one factor experiments. In addition to main effect, the factorial design also allows us to test simple effect.

For example we have 2×2 design. One factor A has two levels A1 and A2 and other factor B has two levels B1 and B2. Main effects compare differences among the level of one factor averaged across all levels of the other. However, this particular design consists of four one way experiment and we may analyse each of them separately. We may be interested in effect of A (all two levels) specifically for condition B2. Simple effects refer to the results of this one factor analysis. To make such comparison the interaction must first be significant.

## 34. Explain the different types of Factorial Design?

Factorial experiments may be conducted either within subject or between subjects.
A mixed factorial design is also used in psychology. A mixed factorial design is one that has at least one within subject variable and at least one between subject variable.

### A) <u>Within Subject Factorial Design</u>

In an experiment by Godden & Baddeley (1975), researcher wants to study the effect of context on memory. They hypothesised that memory should be better when the condition at test are more similar to the conditions experienced during learning.
To operationalise this idea Godden and Baddeley decided to use a very particular population: deepsea divers.

The divers were asked to learn a list of 50 unrelated words either on the beach or under 10 feet of water. The divers were then tested either on beach or under sea. The divers were tested in both the environment in order to make sure that any effect observed could not be attributed to a global effect of one of the environment. The first independent variable is the place of learning. It has 2 levels (on the beach and undersea). The second independent variable is the place of testing. It has two levels (on the beach and undersea). These 2 independent variables gives 4 experimental conditions :

i) Learning on the beach and recalling on the beach.
ii) Learning on the beach and recalling under sea.
iii) Learning under sea and recalling on the beach.
iv) Learning under sea and recalling under sea.

Each subject in this experiment was tested in all four experimental conditions.

The list of words was randomly created and assigned to each subject. The order of testing was randomised in order to control the carry over effect. The layout of the within subject factorial design is presented below.

**Table 2.5: A within subject factorial design**

| Testing Place B | learning place A | |
| --- | --- | --- |
| | Onland $A_1$ | Under Sea $A_2$ |
| $B_1$ | $S_1$ $S_2$ $S_3$ $S_4$ $S_5$ $S_6$ | $S_1$ $S_2$ $S_3$ $S_4$ $S_5$ $S_6$ |
| $B_2$ | $S_1$ $S_2$ $S_3$ $S_4$ $S_5$ $S_6$ | $S_1$ $S_2$ $S_3$ $S_4$ $S_5$ $S_6$ |

## B) __Between Subject Factorial Design__

A between subject factorial design is presented in the following table. The example is 2×2 design. Separate groups of six experiences each condition, thus requiring 24 subjects to get six responses to each of four conditions.

Table 2.6: A between subject factorial design

| Factor-B | Factor - A | |
|---|---|---|
| | $A_1$ | $A_2$ |
| $B_1$ | $S_1$<br>$S_2$<br>$S_3$<br>$S_4$<br>$S_5$<br>$S_6$ | $S_{13}$<br>$S_{14}$<br>$S_{15}$<br>$S_{16}$<br>$S_{17}$<br>$S_{18}$ |
| $B_2$ | $S_7$<br>$S_8$<br>$S_9$<br>$S_{10}$<br>$S_{11}$<br>$S_{12}$ | $S_{19}$<br>$S_{20}$<br>$S_{21}$<br>$S_{22}$<br>$S_{23}$<br>$S_{24}$ |

## C) Mixed Factorial Design

Sometime the researcher uses mixed factorial design. Researcher has two independent variable A and B. Variable A is the within subject variable and variable B is the between subject variable. Subject either experiences B1, once with A1 and also with A2; or they experience B2 once with A1 and also with A2.

For example we want to study the effect of gender and alcohol on risk taking while driving. Here we have two independent variables gender (A) and alcohol level (B). Suppose we have decided to operationalise the independent variable 'alcohol level' by having four concentration levels. We decide to have each subject observed in each alcohol condition. The order of administration of each condition will be randomised for each subject.

121

The measures are non-repeated for the factor (A) Gender and repeated for the factor (B) Alcohol level.

Suppose we have 10 subjects 5 males and 5 females. The experimental lay out will be as follows:

Table 2.7

| Between Subject Variables | Within Subject Variable | | | |
|---|---|---|---|---|
| A | $B_1$ | $B_2$ | $B_3$ | $B_4$ |
| A₁ | $S_1$ $S_2$ $S_3$ | $S_1$ $S_2$ $S_3$ | $S_1$ $S_2$ $S_3$ | $S_1$ $S_2$ $S_3$ |
| | $S_4$ $S_5$ | $S_4$ $S_5$ | $S_4$ $S_5$ | $S_4$ $S_5$ |
| A₂ | $S_6$ $S_7$ $S_8$ $S_9$ $S_{10}$ | $S_6$ $S_7$ $S_8$ $S_9$ $S_{10}$ | $S_6$ $S_7$ $S_8$ $S_9$ $S_{10}$ | $S_6$ $S_7$ $S_8$ $S_9$ $S_{10}$ |

### *Advantage of Factorial Design*:

Factorial design enables the researcher to manipulate and control two or more independent variables simultaneously. By this design we can study the separate and combined effect of number of independent variables.

Factorial design is more precise than single factor design (Kerlinger, 2007).

By factorial design we can find out the independent or main effect of independent variables and interactive effect of two or more independent variables.

The experimental results of a factorial experiment are more comprehensive and can be generalised to a wider range due to the manipulation of several independent variables is one experiment.

***Limitations of Factorial Design***:
Sometime especially when we have more than three independent variables each with three or more levels are to be manipulated together, the experimental setup and statistical analysis become very complicated.

In factorial experiments when the number of treatment combinations or treatments becomes large, it becomes difficult for the experimenter to select a homogeneous group.

## 35. Elaborate the different types of Quasi Experimental Design?

The word quasi means 'as if' or 'to a degree'. Thus quasi experimental design is the one that resembles an experiment but lacks at least one of its defining characteristics.

According to Mcburney & White (2007) 'quasi experiment is a research procedure in which the scientist must select subjects for different conditions from pre-existing groups'.

According to Broota (1989) "All such experimental situations in which the experimenter does not have full control over the assignment of experimental units randomly to the treatment conditions or the treatment cannot be manipulated are called quasi experimental design."

According to Singh (1998) "A quasi experimental design is one that applies an experimental interpretation to results that do not meet all the requirement of a true experiment."

According to Wikipedia, The quasi experimental design are related to the setting up a particular type of an experiment or other study in which one has little or no control over the allocation of the treatment or other factors being studied.

According to Shadish, Cook & Cambell (2002), "The term quasi experimental design refers to a type of research design that lacks the element of random assignment."

Quasi experimental designs are sometimes called ex-post facto design or after the fact experiment, because the experiment is conducted after the groups have been formed. The independent variable has already occurred and hence, the experimenter studies the effect after the occurrence of the variable.
For example if we are interested in gender differences in verbal learning figures we would have to conduct a quasi-experiment because we cannot assign participant to the two conditions male and female. We cannot create groups of males and females but instead select members from pre-existing groups. In other words, we can say that in quasi experiments we do not manipulate variables but we

observe categories of subjects. Matching instead of randomisation is used.

In true experimental situation experimenter has complete control over the experiment. In quasi experimental situation, the experimenter does not have control over the assignment of subject to condition.

In true experimental design we manipulate variables but in quasi experimental design manipulation of variable is not possible, we observe categories of subjects.

For example, if we want to study the effect of gender then we cannot manipulate gender we simply label groups according to what we think is the important difference between them.

In quasi experimental design we present some independent variables to two pre-existing groups. We may not know whether the difference in behaviour was caused by difference between the groups or by the independent variable. A quasi experiment leaves open the possibility that other differences exist between the experimental and control conditions and thus permit other potential differences to remain.

## Types of Quasi Experimental Design:

There are many different types of quasi experimental designs that have a variety of applications in specific context. Here we will study some important quasi experimental designs.

### A)  <u>Non-Equivalent Group, Post-test only Design</u>

The non-equivalent, post-test only design consists of administering an outcome measure to two groups or to a program/treatment group and a comparison.

For example, one group of students might receive reading instruction using a whole language program while the other group of students receives a phonetics based program. After twelve weeks, a reading comprehension test can be administered to see which program was more effective.

A major problem with this design is that the two groups might not be necessarily the same before any instruction takes place and may differ in important ways that influence what reading progress they are able to make. For instance, if it is found that the students in the phonetics groups perform better, there is no way of determining if they are better prepared or better readers even before the program and/or whether other factors are influential to their better performance.

### B)  <u>Non-Equivalent Control Group Design</u>

In this design both a control group and an experimental group is compared.

However the groups are chosen and assigned out of convenience rather than through randomisation. The problem with this design is in determining how to compare results between the experimental and control group.

For example, we are interested to study the effect of special training programmes, on the grade point average of 10th grade students. The experimenter could not draw random sample as the school will not permit the experimenter to regroup the classes.

Therefore researcher selected two sections of X grade from the same school.

Because the subjects were not randomly allocated to the two groups we cannot say that groups are equivalent before the experimental manipulation was performed.

We find out the grade point at the start of the programme and then again after the program. The group who does not receive treatment (training) is our control group.

This design may be diagrammed as shown below:
G1 O1 O2
G2 O3 O4

O = Observation
X = Treatment or experimental variable

Here we cannot say whatever difference we find in the grade point of two groups is because of training programme or because of some other confounding variable.

It is possible that the student of one section who participates in training programme were inherently different in terms of motivation abilities, intelligence from those who did not participate.

## C) The Separate Pre-test -Post-test Sample Design

The basic idea in this design is that the people we use for the pre-test are not the same as the people we use for pre-test. The design may be diagrammed as shown below:


G 1 0
G1 X 0
G2 0
G2 0


There are four groups but two of these one groups come from a single non-equivalent group and the other two also come from other single non-equivalent group.

For example let us say, you have two organisations that you think are similar. You want to implement your study in one organisation and use other as a control. You design a program to improve customer satisfaction. Because customers routinely cycle through your organisation, you cannot measure the same customer pre-post. Instead you measure customer satisfaction in each organisation at one point in time, then implement your program and then once again measure customer satisfaction in the organisation at another point in time after the program. Here the customers will be different within each organisation for the pre-test and post-test. Here we cannot match the individual participant responses from pre to post. We can only look at the change in average customer satisfaction. Here non-equivalence exists not only between the organisations but that is within organisation the pre and post groups are non-equivalent.

### D)  The Double Pre-Test Design

 This is a very strong quasi experimental design with respect to internal validity.

Because in pre-post non-equivalent group design the non-equivalent groups may be different in some way before the program is given and we may incorrectly attribute post-test differences to the program. Although the pre-test helps to assess the degree of pre-program similarity, it does not tell us if the groups are changing at similar rates prior to the program.

The double pre-test design includes two measures prior to the program.
Consequently if the program and comparison group are maturing at different rates we can detect this as a change from pre-test 1 to pre-test 2. Therefore this design explicitly controls for selection maturation threats.

### E)  The Switching Replications Design
The Switching Replications quasi-experimental design is also very strong with respect to internal validity. And, because it allows for two independent implementations of the program, it may enhance external validity or generalisability. The design has two groups and three phases of measurement.

In the first phase of the design, groups are pretested, one is given the program and both are post-tested.

In the second phase of the design, the original comparison group is given the program while the original program group serves as the "control". This design is identical in structure to its randomised experimental version, but lacks the random assignment to group. It is certainly superior to the simple pre-post non-equivalent groups design.

### F) <u>Mixed Factorial Design with one Non-Manipulated Variable</u>

This design can be explained by an experiment. In an experiment Edmund Keogh and Gerke Witt (2001) hypothesise that caffeine intake might influence the perception of pain and that the effect may be different in men and women. 25 men and 25 women took part in two sessions separated by a week. In one session the participants drank a cup of coffee that contained caffeine and in the other session, they drank decaffeinated coffee. In both the sessions the participants put their non-dominant hand in ice water bath and to indicate the point of just noticeable pair.

### G) Interrupted Time-Series Designs

These are the research designs that allow the same group to be compared over time by considering the trend of the data before and after experimental manipulation. (Mcburney & White, 2007).

In this design pre-testing and post-testing of one group of subject is done at different intervals. In the time series design, the purpose might be to determine the long term effect of treatment and therefore the number of pre-test and post-test can vary from one

each to many. Sometimes there is an interruption between
tests in order to assess the strength of treatment over an extended time period.

This design can be diagrammed as below:
01 02 03 04 X 05 06 07 08

The above diagram shows that a series of pre-tests are given to a group. Then treatment (X) is given and a series of post-tests are given to the same subject.
This design is different from single group pre-test post-test design. In this we give the series of pre-tests and post-tests to a subject, where as in the pre-test post-test design we give only single pre-test and post-test.

## H)  <u>Multiple Time Series Design</u>

In this design we have two groups, one group receives treatment and the other group does not receive the treatment and this group acts as the control group.

This design can be presented as given in the  diagram below :

| Pre response measure | Treatment | Post response measure |
|---|---|---|
| $G_1\ 0_1\ 0_2\ 0_3\ 0_4\ 0_5$ | X | $0_6\ 0_7\ 0_8\ 0_9\ 0_{10}$ |
| $G_2\ 0_1\ 0_2\ 0_3\ 0_4\ 0_5$ |  | $0_6\ 0_7\ 0_8\ 0_9\ 0_{10}$ |

It is usually a complex setting with many events and trends that might affect the behaviour in question. The addition of a comparison group for which the same series of measures is available, but which is not exposed to the treatment whose effects are being studied, can be useful in clarifying the relationship between the treatment and any change in the series of behavioural measures being used.

## I)   **Repeated Treatment Design**

Repeated treatment design is one in which a treatment is withdrawn and then presented the second time (McBurney and White, 2007).

In this design the treatment is presented more than once. The subject's response is measured before and after the introduction of a treatment, then the treatment is withdrawn and the whole process is began again. The design is shown in following table:

**Table : A Repeated treatment design**

| Pretest$_1$ | Treatment | Posttest$_1$ | Withdraw | Treatment | Pretest$_1$ | Posttest$_2$ |
|---|---|---|---|---|---|---|

Repeated treatment design can be explained with the help of a study of the effect of a ban on alcohol consumption in a small community, let us say the Today Community in Tamil Nadu. Let us assume that the government has put a ban on alcohol consumption as it is detrimental to the health of the workers in that area.

To assess the impact of alcohol policy changes on the productivity of the workers, medical problems related to alcohol consumption etc., were studied. The results indicated that the productivity improved as a result of this ban amongst the community persons.

## J)   **Counter Balanced Design**

Such designs are also called cross-over design (Cochran & Cox, 1957). The name counter balance was given by Underwood (1949). In this design the experimental control is achieved by randomly applying experimental treatment.

Here each treatment appears once and only once in each column and in each row. A counter balance design in which four treatment have been randomly given to four groups on four different occasion is given below:

| Group-A | $X_1$ | $X_2$ | $X_3$ | $X_4$ | 0 |
| Group-B | $X_2$ | $X_4$ | $X_1$ | $X_3$ | 0 |
| Group-C | $X_3$ | $X_1$ | $X_4$ | $X_2$ | 0 |
| Group-D | $X_4$ | $X_3$ | $X_2$ | $X_1$ | 0 |

Variables like maturation, selection and experimental mortality posing threats to internal validity are well controlled by the counter balance design.

## Advantages and Disadvantages of Quasi – Experimental Design:

### Advantages

In social science, where pre selection and randomisation of groups is often difficult, they can be very useful in generating results for general trends.

E.g. if we study the effect of maternal alcohol use when the mother is pregnant, we know that alcohol does harm embryos. A strict experimental design would include that mothers were randomly assigned to drink alcohol. This would be highly illegal because of the possible harm the study might do to the embryos.

So what researchers do is to ask people how much alcohol they used in their pregnancy and then assign them to groups.

Quasi-experimental design is often integrated with individual case studies; the figures and results generated often reinforce the findings in a case study, and allow some sort of statistical analysis to take place.

In addition, without extensive pre-screening and randomisation needing to be undertaken, they do reduce the time and resources needed for experimentation.

Since quasi-experimental designs are used when randomisation is impossible and/or impractical, they are typically easier to set up than true experimental designs.

Utilising quasi-experimental designs minimises threats to external validity as natural environments do not suffer the same problems of artificially as compared to a well-controlled laboratory setting.

Since quasi-experiments are natural experiments, findings in one may be applied to other subjects and settings, allowing for some generalisations to be made about population.

This experimentation method is efficient in longitudinal research that involves longer time periods which can be followed up in difference environments.

Quasi-experimental design is often integrated with individual case studied; the figures and results generated often reinforce the findings in a case study, and allow some sort of statistical analysis to take place.

In addition, without extensive pre-screening and randomisation needing to be undertaken, they do reduce the time and resources needed for experimentation.

## Disadvantages

Without proper randomisation, statistical tests can be meaningless.

A quasi experiment constructed to analyse the effects of different educational programs on two groups of children, for example, might generate results that show that one program is more effective than the other. These results will not stand up to rigorous statistical scrutiny because the researcher also needs to control other factors that may have affected the results.

The lack of random assignment in the quasi experimental design method may allow studies to be more feasible, but this also poses many challenges for the investigator in terms of internal validity. This deficiency in randomisation makes it harder to rule out confounding variables and introduces new threats to internal validity.

Because randomisation is absent, some knowledge about the data can be approximated, but conclusions of causal relationships are difficult to determine due to a variety of extraneous and confounding variables that exist in a social environment.

Moreover, even if these threats to internal validity are assessed, causation still cannot be fully established because the experimenter does not have total control over extraneous variables.

Thus one may conclude that disadvantages aside, as long as the shortcomings of the quasi experimental design are recognised, these studies can be a very powerful tool, especially in situations where 'true' experiments are not possible.

These are very useful to obtain a general overview and then follow up with a case study or quantitative experiment so as to focus on the underlying reasons for the results generated. They are very useful methods for measuring social variables.

## 36. Enumerate the different types of Correlation Research Design?

Correlation research is a form of descriptive research concerned with determining the extent of relationship existing between variables.

Correlational research designs are founded on the assumption that reality is best described as a network of interacting and mutually causal relationship. Everything affects and is affected by everything else. This web of relationship is not linear.

Thus, the dynamics of a system that is how each part of the whole system affects each other part is more important than causality. The correlational investigations attempt to compare the level of one variable with those of another to see if a relationship exists between the two. The correlational design is a quantitative design.

According to Singh, (1998), Correlational design is one in which the researcher collects two or more sets of data from the same group of subjects so that the relationship between the two subsequent sets of data can be determined.

Correlational research design is one which studies relationship among variables, none of which may be the actual cause of the other (Mcburney & White, 2007).

The correlational design may be diagrammed as follows:

X1 X2
O1 P1
O2 P2
O3 P3
. .

. .
.On Pn

The relationship indicated by the symbol r will be the relationship between the observations (O1 ….On) of X1 and (P1….Pn ) of X2.

**Types of Correlation Research Design:**

Correlational designs can be broadly categorised in two broad divisions:
1) Those that measure the degree of association between variables and
(2) Those that are used to predict the score on one variable using knowledge about the one or more variables.

Within the former, that is those that measure the degree of association between variables, we have (a) Association between two variables and
(b) Association amongst more than 2 variables.

For example let us say a researcher wants to study the relationship between academic stress and academic achievement of college students. For this let us say that the researcher randomly selects 100 college students and administers the measure of academic stress and subsequently a test of academic achievement. Thus the researcher will have two sets of data.

## a) Association between two variables

A correlation coefficient can be calculated from those 100 pairs of numbers.

Theoretically it could take a positive or negative absolute value between - 1.00 to 0.00 to +1.00.

The larger the coefficient, whether positive or negative, the more consistent the relationship between the two variables.

If the coefficient takes a positive value it means the individual who is higher on one variable ($X_1$) will higher on second variable ($X_2$). This is sometimes referred to as a *direct relationship*. If the coefficient takes a negative value between 0 and -1.00, it would indicate that those who have obtained higher scores on $X_1$ will have lower scores on $X_2$. In our above example if the correlation is negative it means that those who scored high on academic stress will have low academic achievement. This is some time referred to as an *inverse relationship.*

## b) Association between more than two variables

So what if academic stress and academic achievement have significant correlation? And what if study habits, intelligence and other factors were also associated with academic achievement. We could measure the association between all these variables in the same group of children. We administer tests for the measurement of study habit and intelligence and obtain scores on the same group of subjects and find out the multiple correlations.

2) Those that are used to predict the score on one variable using knowledge about the one or more variables.

If there is a correlation between two variables, and we know the score on one, the second score can be predicted. In this type of situation there are two variables, one variable that is used to make a forecast about an outcome is known as *predictor variable* and the other variable, is what we are trying to predict is known as *criterion variable.*

By way of regression analysis we can make this prediction. For example there is a relationship between stress and health. If we know the stress score, by way of regression analysis we can predict the future health status score.

Sometime the researchers have more than one predictor variable and one criterion variable. The combination gives us more power to make accurate predictions. for example if we have stress scores as well as health behaviour score and past health score then one can make more accurate prediction of health status. Here we have three predictors, stress, health behaviour and previous health status and one criterion variable future health.

**Evaluation of Correlation Design:**

First we deal with advantage and then the disadvantages.

### *Advantages:*

The correlational designs are used in many cases because available data makes it easy to use. Some more careful researchers use the result of correlational studies to formulate new hypothesis which they can test later using more rigorous research design rather than test hypothesis about cause and effect directly.

Correlational design is used as the foundation for other designs that permit more certain causal inferences to be drawn from results.

It usually does not involve repeated administration of a behavioural measure, thus avoiding pre-test sensitisation.

It usually uses very realistic measurements of behaviour and its possible causes as well.

Correlational research thus avoids the problem of non-representative research context. It also permits the use of large carefully chosen sample thus avoiding the threat of non-representative sample of participant.

### *Disadvantages*

The major disadvantage of correlational designs is that they leave the actual

reason for the association found quite unclear. For example there is a positive

correlation between exposure to violent program on television and violence on

the playground. If we find the correlation rather positive and high, we may be tempted to conclude that exposure to violent television causes children to be aggressive and violent. But such a conclusion is completely unwarranted.

Correlational designs have directional problem. The causation is reversed from the expected direction. The designation of one of the variables as the independent variable and one as the dependent variable is arbitrary compared to a true experiment, in which the independent variable is manipulated by the researcher.

Children may watch violent television program because they behave aggressively rather than the other way round. Television program may validate their choice of activities by showing others who do the same, or children may watch to learn more about how to behave violently.

## 37. Discuss the different types of Qualitative Research?

Qualitative research helps in providing an in depth knowledge regarding human behaviour and tries to find out reasons behind decision making tendencies of humans.

Qualitative research can be defined as a type of scientific research that tries to bridge the gap of incomplete information, systematically collects evidence, produces findings and thereby seeks answer to a problem or question. It is widely used in collecting and understanding specific information about the behaviour, opinion, values and other social aspects of a particular community, culture or population.

An example of a qualitative research can be studying the concepts of spiritual development amongst college students.

Qualitative research uses observation as the data collection method. Observation is the selection and recording of behaviors of people in their environment. Observation is used extensively in studies by psychologists, anthropologists, sociologists and programme evaluators.

**Types of Qualitative Research:**

Creswell (1998) has categorised Qualitative research in context of their forms, terminologies and focus as follows:

i)     **Case study:** With the help of this method a case of an individual, group, event, institution or society is studied. It helps in providing an in depth knowledge of the nature, process or phenomena of a specific case under study. Multiple methods of data collection are often used in case study research (example, interviews, observation, documents, and questionnaires).

The final report of the case study provides a rich (i.e., vivid and detailed) and holistic (i.e., describes the whole and its parts) description of the case and its context.

ii) **Ethnography:** This approach mainly focuses on a particular community. It is more of a kind of close field observation and basically tries to study socio cultural phenomena. For example, judging others based on the researchers' cultural standards. Ethnography can be used for comparative analysis of cultural groups (e.g. eating habits of North Indians and South Indians), also known 'Ethnology'. Further it can also be used to analyse the cultural past of group of people (e.g. Harrapan civilisation), also known as 'Ethno history'.

iii) **Historical method:** This method helps in understanding and analysing the causal relationships. With the help of this technique, the data related to the occurrence of an event is collected and evaluated in order to understand the reasons behind occurrence of such events. It helps in testing hypothesis concerning cause, effects and trends of events that may help to explain present events and anticipate future events as well.

iv) **Grounded theory:** This approach involves an active participation of the researcher in the activities of the group, culture or the community under study. The data regarding the required information is collected with the help of observation. It is generally used in generating or developing theories. This means that the ground theorists can not only work upon generation of new theories, they can test or elaborate previously grounded theories.

v) **Phenomenology:** In this method, the behavioural phenomenon is explained with the help of conscious experience of events, without using any theory, calculations or assumptions from other disciplines.it focus on describing all participants have in common, as they experience a phenomena.

## 38. What are the differences between Qualitative and Quantitative researches?

Differences between qualitative and quantitative research on the basis of purpose and focus, units of analysis, type of data, methods of data collection, results and analysis as follows:

|  | Qualitative Research | Quantitative Research |
| --- | --- | --- |
| General Frame work: | Seeks to explore phenomena using some structured methods such as in depth interviews, experiences, participant observation. | Seeks to confirm hypothesis related to phenomena using highly structured methods such as, questionnaires, surveys, structured observation. |
| Objectives: | It aims to describe variation, explain relationships, describe behaviour, experiences and norms of individuals and groups. | It aims to quantify variation, predict causal relationships. |
| Questions: | The questions used for data collection are open ended ones | The questions used for data collection are close ended ones |
| Representation of data: | Data is represented in form of notes, recordings and video tapes. | Data is represented in form of numbers and graphs. |
| Research Design: | The research design allows some flexibility in certain situational aspects. The questions used for the data collection differs individually and depends upon the response of the participants. | The research design is predetermined and stable from the beginning. The questions used for data collection are structured and same for all the participants. |

In Qualitative research, Data is analysed by systematically organising and interpreting information using categories, themes and motifs that identify patterns and relationships while in Quantitative research, data analysis is done using standardised statistics and procedures.

Results are in-depth explanations for patterns of behaviours in Qualitative research while in case of Quantitative research, results tend to summarise patterns of similarities, size, direction, etc.

## 39. Write a short note on Ethnography?

Ethnography is defined by Spradley and McCurdy as "The task of describing a particular culture" as the predominant method used by cultural anthropologists interested in relatively primitive cultures. It focuses on studying socio cultural phenomena of a community.

The ethnographer/ researcher collect information regarding the socio cultural phenomena from a lot of people belonging to the community under study.

On behalf of their community, the participants also identify and provide the researcher some more respondents as a representative of their community (also known as chaining process). The data is therefore collected using a chain sampling in all empirical areas of investigation. The selected samples are re- interviewed in order to elicit deeper and ambiguous responses.

The ethnographer stays within the community for months in order to gain more information through chaining process and collect data in form of observational transcripts and interview recordings. The analysis of data leads to development of theories for the socio cultural phenomena under study, only on basis of the views and perspectives of its respondents.

**Common terms used by Ethnographers**:

i)     **Symbols:** Symbols refers to any tradition or material artifact of a particular culture such as art, clothing, food, technology and rituals. The ethnographer tries to understand the cultural connotations behind the symbols of a particular culture.

ii)     **Cultural patterning:** Ethnographic research believes that the meaning of symbols cannot be understood until it is paired with one or more symbols.

Cultural patterning refers to the study of cultural patterns formed through relationships between two or more than two symbols.

iii) **Tacit knowledge:** It refers to those cultural beliefs which are firm in nature.

They are so deeply embedded in their culture that they rarely need to be discussed by the members in an explicit way. Such knowledge cannot be observed but needs to be inferred by the ethnographer e.g. the prejudices or the orthodox beliefs).

iii)     **Situational reduction:** It refers to the belief of ethnographers that social structures and social dynamism are a result of interactions of several social situations (e.g criminal acts can be due to the poor economic condition, frustration, parenthood, neighbours and peer group of the criminals).

**<u>Assumptions in Ethnography</u>:**

i) Ethnographic research assumes that the main objective of research depends upon and is affected by the interpretation of community cultural understandings. There are chances that the researcher over estimates the role of cultural perception and underestimates the role of causal reasons behind such cultural belief.

ii) It also assumes that it is very important as well as difficult to identify the target community that requires to be studied by the researcher. Nature and size of the community as well as individuals' perception may play an important role on the subject that needs to be studied. Chances exist that the ethnographer may overestimate the role of community culture and underestimate the causal role of individual beliefs and perceptions.

iii) Ethnography further assumes that that the researcher is an expert and is thorough with the norm and mores of the culture. The researcher is also assumed to be an expert in the language spoken in the community. Chances exist that the researcher may show biasness towards his or her culture while studying the population of another community.

## Types of Ethnographic Research:

i) **Macro ethnography:** It is the study of broadly defined cultural groupings such as – "the Indians", "the Turkish". The common perspectives are studied at a more larger level, which are found to be common under a more broader strata.

ii) **Micro ethnography:** It is the study of more specific cultural groupings such as the "local government", the "terrorists".

iii) **Emic perspectives:** It is the ethnographic approach under which the view points and responses of the 'ingroup' or the members of the culture under study are noted down.

iv) **Etic perspective:** It is the ethnographic approach under which the view points and responses of the 'out groups' or the members who do not belong to the culture under study are noted down. Their viewpoints highlight the phenomena being followed under a particular culture.

## Purpose of Ethnographic Research:

It helps in cross cultural analysis.

It helps in analysing the past events or the history of the culture.

It helps in studying the behaviour, experiences and attitudes of individuals in a more natural environment. Close observation increases the chances of validity in the reports and theory formulated.

## Steps of Ethnographic Method:

1) **Selection:** The ethnographic method begins with selection of a culture. The researcher selects the culture/ community or population according to his or her interest.

2) **Review of Literature:** Then the researcher reviews the literature pertaining to the culture to get a brief idea and historical sketch of the culture selected for study.

3) **Identification of variables:** The researcher then identifies variables which interests him or her as well as the members of the culture and needs to be explored.

4) **Entry:** The ethnographer then tries to enter the culture and gain the acceptance of the members of the culture.

5) **Cultural Immersion:** Ethnographers live in the culture for months or even years which they have chosen to study. The middle stages of the ethnographic method involve gaining informants, using them to gain yet more informants in a chaining process.

6) **Data Collection:** After gaining the confidence of the respondents, the researcher collects information in form of observational transcripts and interview recordings and tapings.

7) **Development of theory:** After analysing the data, the researcher formulates theory on the basis of interpretation of the results and reports achieved.

## 40. Write a short note on "Steps of Grounded Theory"?

Grounded theory is a general methodology used to develop new concepts or theories through data that have been obtained and analysed in an ongoing, systematic manner.

Grounded theory is one of the basic approach and most prominently used technique in qualitative research.

Grounded theory refers to 'the process of generation of theory which is based on collection of data from multiple sources'.

It is the only method of qualitative research which uses quantitative data also, as and when required. The grounded theory approach aims to collect data and interpret the data from the textual base (for example, a collection of field notes or video recordings). After the process of interpreting, the data base is categorised into different variables and then the interrelationship between these variables are analysed and studied.

Grounded theory provides a direction to the researcher and directs them to generate new theories or modify the existing ones. The interpretation and conclusion of the grounded theory approach is more reliable as it is based on data collected from multiple sources. The theory takes similar cases for analysis rather than variable perspective.

The *basic goals* of the grounded theory are:

i) Since the approach consists of a series of systematic steps and the data is collected from more than one source, it assures to provide a 'good theory' as the output.

ii) The grounded theory approach emphasises on the process by which the theory is evaluated. This determines the quality of the theory.

iii) The grounded theory approach also emphasises on enhancing the theoretical sensitivity.

iv) One goal of a grounded theory is to formulate hypotheses based on conceptual ideas.

v) On the basis of the questions asked the researcher tries to discover the participants' main concern and how they continually try to resolve it.

vi) It also aims to generate those concepts which explain people's actions regardless of time and place. The descriptive parts of a GT are there mainly to illustrate the concepts.

In the words of Glaser (1998), "GT (grounded theory) is multivariate. It happens sequentially, subsequently, simultaneously, serendipitously, and scheduled".

## Methods of Grounded Theory:

Unlike other methods of qualitative research, the grounded theorists do not believe in collecting data through taping and transcribing interviews as it is believed to be a waste of time in grounded theories. The process of grounded theories is far quick and faster as the researcher delimits the data by field-noting interviews and soon after generates concepts that fit with data, are relevant and work in explaining what participants are doing to resolve their main concern.

**Steps of Grounded Theory**:

Grounded theory approach helps in generating theories on the basis of the following systematic steps

## A) Memoing
The first objective of the researcher is to collect data in form of memos. Memos are a form of short notes that the researcher writes and prepares. These memos act as a source of data which is further put in other processes of analysis and interpretation. These short notes or memos can be prepared in three ways:

a) *Theoretical note*
This form of note contains the details regarding how a textual data basis related to the existing literature of the concerned study. The note consists of about one to five pages, Anyhow, the final theory and report consists of an integration of several such theoretical notes.

b) *Field note*
Field note consists of the notes prepared when the researcher actively participates with the population/ culture or the community under study. It can be the observations of behaviours, interactions, events or

situations that occur on the spot and it also contains the causal notes behind such actions.

c) *Code notes*

The researcher or the ground theorist may also prepare notes by naming, labelling or categorising things, properties and events. The code notes are those notes which discuss the codes of such labelling. These code notes further acts as a source of formation of final reports. Further, these code notes also acts as a guide to the ground theorists while analysing a text or a case.

## B) Sorting in Grounded Theory

Once the short notes or the memos are prepared, the collected information (or the data) is sorted in order to organise them in proper order. Sorting helps in putting all the data in proper order which leads to proper linkage of information and ideas.

## C) Writing in Grounded Theory

After the memos are sorted, the next stage towards preparation of theory is "writing". The ground theorist arranges, relates and puts the collected information into words. Therefore, in this step the researcher tries to give a shape as well as meaning to the relevant data. This may be said to be a crucial stage, as it is this stage in which the researcher interprets the information on the basis of his own perspectives.

## 41. What are the different types of Coding in Grounded Theory?

Ground theorists analyse and categorise events and try to identify the meaning of the text with the help of the prepared code notes. Preparation of the code notes can be done in three ways-

### A) Selective Coding
In this type of coding out of all the available categories, the ground theorist selects one category to be the centre or the major one and then tries to relate the other categories with the selected major category.

### B) Open Coding
It is the process of identifying, labelling and analysing the phenomena found in the text. The ground theorist on the basis of generalisation categorises names, events or properties in to more general categories or dimensions.

### C) Axial Coding
It is the process of relating the categories or properties (that is the codes) to each other with the help of deductive and inductive thinking. The ground theorists try to analyse the causal relations between these variables, that is, which of the code is the 'cause' which has led to the occurrence of other codes- the 'context'. The ground theorist analyses and interprets the cause' codes and the 'context' codes without showing much interest on the 'consequences' of the phenomenon itself.

## 42. Write a short note on "Discourse Analysis"?

The term 'discourse analysis' has its origin since 1960s, and is prominently being used in interdisciplinary fields, basically refers to the explanation of the researchers or analysts in form of talks or texts.

Discourse analysis is a generic term covering a heterogeneous number of theoretical approaches and analytical constructs.

Discourse analysis has been defined in different ways. Some of the basic definitions are as follows:

In the words of Hammersley, M. (2002) It is a study of the way versions or the world, society, events and psyche are produced in the use of language and discourse. The Semiotics, deconstruction and narrative analysis are forms of discourse analysis.

Bernard Berelson defined content analysis as "a research technique for the objective, systematic, and quantitative description of manifest content of communications" (Berelson,1974). It can also be defined as an analysis of speech units larger than the sentence and of their relationship to the contexts in which they are used.

### Assumptions of Discourse Analysis:

Theoretically discourse analysis is an interdisciplinary approach and has been widely used by the social scientists and cognitive psychologists. Some of the basic assumption of this approach can be outlined as follows:

a) Psychologists assume that the human behaviour can only be studied with objectivity that is, without involvement of any biasness or subjectivity of the researcher as well as the subject/people under study. However, this has been disputed – people, including researchers, cannot be objective.

b) The approach also assumes that, reality is socially constructed. It is assumed in a scientific research that 'reality' can be categorised. The constructs generally used by psychologists like – personality, intelligence and thinking are explained as real and naturally occurring categories or events.

c) It is also assumed that, people are the result of social interaction. In the scientific approach it is assumed that many of the constructs used are 'inner essences'.

That is to say that personality, anxiety, drives, and so on exist somewhere within our heads and our bodies and are revealed only when the individual socially interacts with others.

## Approaches or Theories of Discourse Analysis:

There are numerous "types" or theories of discourse analysis. The various discourses has been explained or categorised on basis of several theories and approaches. Some of them are:

**_Modernism:_** The theorists of modernism were guided by achievement and reality based orientation. Thereby they viewed discourse as being relative to talking or way of talking. They emphasised that the discourse and language transformations are needed to develop new or more "accurate" words in order to describe new inventions, innovations, understandings, or areas of interest. Both language and discourse are now conceptualised as natural or real products of common sense usage or progress. Modernism gave rise to various discourses of rights, equality, freedom, and justice.

**_Structuralism_**: The structuralism theorists squabble that the human actions and social formations are related to language and discourse and they can be implicated or considered as systems of related elements. The approach believed that the individual elements of a system only have significance when they are considered in context to the structure as a whole. The structures can be defined as self-contained, self-regulated, and self-transforming entities. In other words, it is the structure itself that determines the significance, meaning and function of the individual elements of a system. Structuralism has made an eminent contribution to the world of language and social systems.

**_Postmodernism_**: Unlike the approaches of the modern theory, the postmodern theorists examined and investigated the variety of experience of individuals and groups and emphasised more on differences over similarities and common experiences. Postmodern researchers insisted more upon analysing discourses as texts, language, policies and practices. In the field of discourse analysis, the most prominent figure was Michel Foucault.

Foucault (1977, 1980) has defined discourse as "systems of thoughts composed of ideas, attitudes, courses of action, beliefs and practices that systematically construct the subjects and the worlds of which they speak." He emphasised that the discourse analysis has a significant role in social processes of legitimating and power.

Foucault (1977, 1980) argued that power and knowledge are inter-related and therefore every human relationship is a struggle and negotiation of power. Discourse according to Foucault (1977, 1980, 2003) is related to power as it operates by rules of exclusion.

*Feminism*: Feminists explained discourse as events of the social practices. They investigated the complex relationships that exist among power, ideology, language and discourse. They emphasised on the concept of 'performing gender'.

## Steps in Discourse Analysis:

The method of discourse analysis evaluates the patterns of speech, such as how people talk about a particular subject, what metaphors they use, how they take turns in conversation, and so on. These analysts see speech as a performance.

The researchers collect and interpret information in the following steps:

i) **_Target orientation_**: First of all, the analysts need to know their target or focus of study. Since beginning, they need to think about the ways by which they will analyse and interpret data after collecting the information.

ii) **_Significance of data_**: Once the relevant information is collected, the **Discourse Analysis** researchers need to judge or examine the value of the collected data, especially those which may have come from more than one source.

iii) **_Interpretation of the data_**: As the research progresses the analyst needs to try to understand and interpret the data so that the researchers as well as others can gain an understanding of what is going on.

iv) **_Analysis of the findings_**: Finally, the researcher needs to undertake the mechanical process of analysing, interpreting and summarising the data collected. On basis of the analysis of the information, the findings can be summarised and concluded. There are many qualitative analysis programs available to social researchers that can be used for a variety of different tasks. For example, software could locate particular words or phrases; make lists of words and put them into alphabetical order; insert key words or comments; count occurrences of words or phrases or attach numeric codes. With the help of the software's, the analysts or the researcher can retrieve text, analyse text and build theories. Although a computer can undertake these mechanical processes, it cannot think about, judge or interpret qualitative data.

## 43. Write a short note on Content Analysis?

Content Analysis one of the method which is used in summarising any form of content only after having a deep study of the actual content. This enables the researcher to more objectively evaluate and understand the situations.

For example, an impressionistic summary of a TV program, cannot help in analysing the over all aspects of the content of the program.

Content analysis, tries to analyse written words. The results of content analysis are numbers and percentages. It starts with the process of selecting content for analysis, then preparing the content for coding. After the content is coded, it is counted and weighed. Later, conclusions are drawn on the basis of the weighing.

The content analysis therefore serves two basic purposes:
i) It helps in removing much of the subjectivity from summaries
ii) It also helps in detection of trends in an easier and simpler manner.

Content analysis can be done with the help of media content (when the sources of media) is being used or audience content (when individual feedbacks are being used). Few of the examples of media content are: print media, broadcasts, and recordings, while the audience content is analysed with the help of questionnaire, interviews, group discussions and letters to the editors.

Content analysis has several implications:

i)     Content analysis enables the researcher to make links between causes (e.g. program content) and effect (e.g. audience size).

ii)     The content analysis is used to evaluate and improve the programming of the media world.

iii)     It also helps in increasing awareness and summarising the various notes or documentaries which focus on a specific issue.

iv)     It also helps in making inferences of the causes.

## 44. What are the steps of evaluating data and the strategies of interpreting data in a qualitative research?

No research is complete without having detailed information of the results or achievements in form of reports of the research survey conducted by the researcher. After the collection of data, the researcher needs to analyse, evaluate and then report data in an organised and systematic way.

After collecting of data through various techniques or methods of research, the researcher tries to find out a solution to a problem, behaviour or uncertain environment. Such a solution or conclusion can be reached only with the help of systematically analysing or evaluating the data or information gathered and then organising the analysis and interpretations in form of reports. Once the data has been collected with the help of questionnaires, interviews, focus groups, or whatever, the data needs to be analysed or evaluated.

The process of evaluating the collected information or the data follows a systematic step. The researcher tries to organise and give meaning to the collected information in such a way, so that there is less chance of bias or confusion.

Following are the steps of the process of evaluating data:
i) Reading the overall collected data
ii) Categorising the collected data
iii) Naming or labelling the categories

iv)  Identification of the causal relationships
v) Recording or filing the data

Let us take up each of these steps and explain.

i)  ***Reading the overall collected data***: Firstly, the researcher tries to go through the details of the information collected through various sources ( for example interviews, video tapes, audio tapes, observation and so on). This step helps in getting as much information as is required regarding the variables which the researcher selects for studying.

ii)  ***Categorising the collected data***: From the collected information, the researcher or the analyst's sort's relevant information, which may have a direct or indirect effect on the behaviour, objects, events or practices selected for the study. After sorting the data, the researcher categorises similar information under various categories or themes, as for example, the researcher may similar experiences, program inputs, recommendations, outputs, outcome indicators, and so on .

iii)  ***Naming or labelling the categories***: The third systematic step in evaluation process of the research is labelling the sorted and categorised themes, for example keeping all the information of suggestions under the category of propositions.

iv) ***Identification of the causal relationships***: With the help of categorising and labelling of information, the researcher gets an idea of the direction or flow of information. This helps the researcher or the analysts to discover patterns, or associations and causal relationships amongst the categorised themes.

For example, if most people of the sample under study belonged to the same geographic area, we may state that people if live in that area may have a certain problem.

v) ***Recording or filing the data***: Once the patterns of relationships are analysed, the analysts need to keep a track or record of the same. These records or files serves as a guide for future reference, while the similar sample is being studied.

Interpretation of data refers to summarising the findings of the data analysis in such a way that it provides useful information related to the goals of research.

The researcher or the analysts attempts to put the information in the form of a viewpoint. For example, the researcher may compare the findings of the results with what was expected in the beginning stage.

# References

D; Amato, M.R. (1970): *Experimental Psychology*. Tokoya : McGraw – Hill.

Grinnell, Richard Jr (ed.) 1988, *Social Work Research and Evaluation* (3rd edition) Itasca, Illinois, F.E. Peacock Publishers.

Kerlinger, F. N. (1979) *Foundation of Behavioural Research*, New York, : H 107, Rinehart and Winstem Inc.

Kuhn, T.S. (1970). *The Structure of Scientific Revolutions* (2nd edition) Chicago: University of Chicago Press.

Kumar. R (2006) *Research Methodology*. New Delhi: Dorling Kingsley

Townsend, J.C. (1953): *Introduction to Experimental Method*. Tokyo: McGraw Hill.

Guilford, J.P. (1954). *Psychometric Methods.* New Delhi: Tata McGraw Hill.

McBurney, D.H. & White, T. L. (2007) *Research Methods*, New Delhi; Akash Press.

Kerlinger, F. N. (1986). *Foundations of Behavioural Research*. New York: Holt Rinehart and Winston.

Postman , L. and Egan, J.P. (1949). *Experimental Psychology.* New York; Harper & Row

Goode, WJ & Hatt, PK (1981). *Methods in Social Research*. Tokyo: McGraw hill Book Company.

Young, PV (1992). *Scientific Social Survey and Research*,New Delhi: Prenticehall of India.

Myers, Anne, & Hansen, Christine. (2006). *Experimental Psychology*. Thomson Wadsworth: Belmont,CA.

Broota, K.D. (1992) *Experimental Design in Behavioural Research*, Wiley Eastern Limited.

DEP-SSA, IGNOU (2008). *A Document of Action Research*, IGNOU, New Delhi.

Cambell, D.T. and Slanley, J.C. (1966), *Experimenal and Quasi Experimental*
*Design for Research*, Chicago : Rand McNally College Pub. Co.

Qyen, E. (ed.) (1990), *Comparative Methodology : Theory and Practice in International Social Research*, London sage.

Agar, Michael (1996). *Professional Stranger: An Informal Introduction to Ethnography*, Second edition. Academic Press, ISBN 0120444704 .

Miles, MB and Huberman AM (1984) *Qualitative Data Analysis, A Sourcebook of New Methods*. Beverley Hills, CA, USA.: Sage Publications.

www.ingramcontent.com/pod-product-compliance
Lightning Source LLC
Chambersburg PA
CBHW040142160726
48006CB00014B/1584